How to Solve True Crime

How to Solve True Crime

Occam's Razor and the Limitations of Simplicity in Investigations

Davina Kaur

PEN & SWORD
TRUE CRIME

First published in Great Britain in 2025 by
Pen & Sword True Crime
An imprint of Pen & Sword Books Limited
Yorkshire – Philadelphia

Copyright © Davina Kaur 2025

ISBN 978 1 39905 711 0

The right of Davina Kaur to be identified as
Author of this Work has been asserted by her in accordance
with the Copyright, Designs and Patents Act 1988.

A CIP catalogue record for this book is
available from the British Library.

Typeset by Mac Style
Printed in the UK by CPI Group (UK) Ltd, Croydon, CR0 4YY.

MIX
Paper | Supporting
responsible forestry
FSC
www.fsc.org   FSC® C013604

The Publisher's authorised representative in the EU for product
safety is Authorised Rep Compliance Ltd., Ground Floor,
71 Lower Baggot Street, Dublin D02 P593, Ireland.
www.arccompliance.com

For a complete list of Pen & Sword titles please contact

PEN & SWORD BOOKS LIMITED
47 Church Street, Barnsley, South Yorkshire, S70 2AS, England
E-mail: enquiries@pen-and-sword.co.uk
Website: www.pen-and-sword.co.uk
or
PEN AND SWORD BOOKS
1950 Lawrence Road, Havertown, PA 19083, USA
E-mail: uspen-and-sword@casematepublishers.com
Website: www.penandswordbooks.com

Due to the graphic nature of these cases, reader discretion is advised. This book includes graphic descriptions and discussions of murder and assault that some people may find disturbing. Extreme caution is advised.

Contents

Image Credits

1. William of Ockham, from stained glass window at a church in Surrey by Moscarlop under Licence Creative Commons Attribution – Share Alike 3.0 Unported
2. Sketch labelled 'frater Occham iste'. Illustration of William of Ockham, from a 1341 manuscript of Ockham's Summa Logicae (MS Gonville and Caius College, Cambridge, 464/571, fol. 69r) under United States Public Domain.
3. Photo of Jane Britton, by Lincoln Studio, Malden MA, USA, available on Page 12 of Middlesex County District Attorney's press packet on the resolution of Jane Britton's homicide investigation
4. Red Ochre by Ahamed Kafir M under licence Creative Commons Attribution – Share Alike 4.0 International
5. Craigie Arms by Daderot released under the Public Domain
6. Jacob Wetterling by Alcatraz East Crime Museum https://www.crimemuseum. org/crime-library/kidnappings/jacob-wetterling/
7. Jacob Wetterling Map by Canadaolympic989 under licence Creative Commons Attribution – Share Alike 4.0 International
8. Jacob Wetterling Grave Site by ApolloHSclass96 under licence Creative Commons Attribution – Share Alike 4.0 International
9. Google Earth, (14 January 2023) MCM Elegante Hotel, 2355 I-10, Beaumont, TX 77705, United States [online] available through https://earth.google.com/ web/search/MCM+elegante+hotel/@30.0529993,-94.1402208,8.46008459a, 899.7645721d,35y,-187.6181997h,0t,0r/data=CigiJgokCV59Y3P6OkRAET X401V8M0RAGUT3B67f6VvAIcZ_7GAj7VvAOgMKATA [02/01/2024]
10. Google Earth, (2/2023) Mount Timpanogos Utah Temple, American Fork, Utah, [online]. .Available through https://earth.google.com/web/search/Moun t+Timpanogos+Utah+Temple/@40.3930005,-111.7704109,1463.45908792a, 781.6848608d,35y,323.99550024h,45t,0r/data=CocBGl0SVwolMHg4NzRk ODEzMGE3ZTc0MjI1OjB4ZTI0OWUxOGYxYmRlMjg2MRnkZyPXT TJEQCHY_oRpTvFbwCocTW91bnQgVGltcGFub2dvcyBVdGFoIFRlbX BsZRgCIAEiJgokCf7M01j7NkRAEQoLaqF-L0RAGeMa1Fpr7VvAIfiiC M3b8lvAOgMKATA [02/01/2024]
11. Google Earth, (28/07/2023), Timpanogos Cave National Monument, East Alpine Loop Road, American Fork, UT, USA, [online]. Available through https://earth.google.com/web/search/Timpanogos+Cave+Na tional+Monument,+East+Alpine+Loop+Road,+American+Fork,+UT,+U SA/@40.4439208,-111.7051436,1720.78297944a,781.03791415d,35y,0h,4

5t,0r/data=Cr0BGpIBEosBCiUweDg3NGQ4NzlmNjdiMDVmMTk6MH
g2ZjM5NmExNTkxY2IzYmViGdABk2XSOERAIfU-nxIh7VvAKlBUaW
1wYW5vZ29zIENhdmUgTmF0aW9uYWwgTW9udW1lbnQsIEVhc3Qg
QWxwaW5lIExvb3AgUm9hZCwgQW1lcmljYW4gRm9yaywgVVQsIFV
TQRgCIAEiJgokCfAa5rA6OkRAEVysiGcMM0RAGZRTEqVF7VvA
Ib_DXjgn8VvAKAI6AwoBMA

12. The Grave of Gareth Wyn Williams (1978 - 2010) in Ynys Wen Cemetery, Valley, Anglesey by Nabokov, under licence Creative Commons Attribution – Share Alike 4.0 International
13. Joseph and Summer McStay with their two young sons, available at San Bernadino County Court under licence Creative Commons Attribution – Share Alike 4.0 International
14. Michael Morton, by Lauren Gerson originally posted to Flicker, licenced under Creative Commons Attribution 2.0 Generic licence.

Acknowledgements

I would like to extend my gratitude to several individuals, in no particular order, whose support was instrumental in bringing this book to fruition.

Firstly, a heartfelt thank you to *Pen and Sword Books* for giving this book a home.

I am deeply grateful to Ally Pennington at the Alcatraz East Crime Museum for generously permitting the use of photographs from the 'Crime Museum'.

Thank you to Olivia Camozzi for your unwavering belief in me throughout this journey and for facilitating my connection with Commissioning Editor Jonathan Wright. Jonathan, your willingness to take a chance on both me and this project means the world.

To Charlotte Mitchell, thank you immensely for diligently addressing every late-night email I sent your way. Told you I would make sure you were in here!

To Lydia Waites, thank you for never hesitating to read and edit my work, no matter what sort of state it is in. I will be sending you chapters to read till we're old and grey.

Thank you to Harrison, for your steadfast support. I'm so grateful that our paths crossed in that university accommodation.

My gratitude extends to my parents – my mother, Asha, for watching Crimewatch in the late evenings when I was younger; I am going to blame my interest in True Crime on you. And to my father, Europe, hopefully, I will be reading my name in an acknowledgement of the book you will write one day. A special mention goes to my siblings, Dillon and Dayna. You are the Gene and Louise to my Tina, and my favourite people in the world. Thank you to all four of you for everything.

And lastly, to you, dear reader, I extend my sincere gratitude for taking a chance on both myself and this book. Thank you.

Introduction

At 12.58 in the afternoon on July 26th, 2009, Warren Hance received a phone call from his 36-year-old sister, Diane Schuler. Expecting his sister's voice, he was shocked to hear the voice of his young daughter. 'There is something wrong with Aunt Diane,' she said.[1]

Warren listened intently as his scared 8-year-old daughter Emma described her Aunt Diane as having trouble seeing while driving and that she was not speaking clearly. Diane took the phone herself and described being disorientated; her vision was foggy.

Panicked, Warren instructed Diane to pull over and stay off the road; he would meet them shortly. But by the time he arrived, Diane had left, and tragedy was on the horizon.

Diane had been camping before this phone call with her husband, Daniel Schuler, their children and nieces at the Hunter Lake Campground in Parksville, New York. They prepared the family to head home to West Babylon that late July day.

The journey began benevolently. Around 9.30 am, Diane and her three nieces, Emma, 7-year-old Alyson, 5-year-old Kate, and her children, 5-year-old son Bryan and 2-year-old daughter Emma, left the camp in her minivan. Daniel followed behind in a truck. Along the route home, the party in the minivan stopped at McDonald's and several gas stations. So far, it seemed like a typical New York family heading home after a camping trip. But bystanders would say otherwise.

As Diane was making her way down the New York Thruway, she called her brother Warren to tell him that the heavy traffic was delaying them, but other motorists reported a minivan driving aggressively on the highway, tailgating, flashing their headlights, honking their horn and straddling two lanes. Other witnesses reported seeing a minivan pulled over on the side of the road with a woman bent over next to it, vomiting.

Warren would receive his daughter's phone call two hours later, and the following series of events would be pieced together through witness statements and toll information.

At 1.33 pm, 911 operators received two separate calls reporting a minivan driving the wrong way up an exit ramp on the Taconic State Parkway; one minute later, 911 operatives received four more calls. This time, depicting a similar van driving the wrong way down the parkway at 80 miles per hour.[2]

The van was Diane's.

For 1.7 miles, the van erratically sped south down the northbound lanes of the Parkway before colliding head-on with a Chevrolet Trailblazer, which subsequently hit a Chevrolet Tracker at 1.35 pm. The entire event took place in less than three minutes.

Seven of the eleven people involved in the crash were pronounced dead at the scene; one would die later at the hospital, bringing the total number of fatalities to eight.

Diane, her daughter and two of her nieces were likely killed instantly. The children had been in the backseat but were not secured in car seats or wearing seatbelts.

The three passengers of the Trailblazer, 81-year-old Michael Bastardi, his 49-year-old son, Guy, and their friend, 74-year-old Dan Longo, were doubtlessly killed on impact. The two passengers in the Tracker received only minor injuries.

Whilst Diane's son and one of her nieces initially survived the crash and were taken to a local hospital, Bryan would suffer from severe head trauma and several broken bones whilst ultimately surviving his ordeal. Unfortunately, the niece would not.

Of course, there was a media frenzy; what happened to this perfect PTA mother that caused her to snap and cause the death of eight people? What caused the worst motor vehicle collision in New York State History?

Liz Garbus, an American documentary film director and producer, strived to capture a more nuanced portrayal of a woman who seemed to have it all. In her documentary, 'There's something wrong with Aunt

Diane.' She tried to piece together the calamity by interviewing Diane's family and friends, Daniel and her sister-in-law, Jay.[3]

Daniel Schuler illustrates Diane as a conscientious mother who strove for perfection and would never knowingly endanger children. He believed his wife must have suffered from a stroke, an aneurysm, or a heart attack that caused her to drive erratically. Daniel sued the state for damages, claiming that the accident resulted from the Taconic's poor design and inadequate signage.[4] You may be interested to know that the lawsuits stemming from the crash have been settled, whilst the terms of the settlements are confidential.[5]

The evidence was stacked against Diane. The odds were not looking good.

Two fellow drivers who witnessed the ordeal were some of the first responders. As soon as they saw what happened, they rushed to help – pulling Diane and her children out of the van. They almost missed Bryan, as his pliant body was buried underneath his siblings and cousins.

As they pulled Diane out, they reported seeing a large bottle of Absolut Vodka on the floor of the driver's side – a report that would be considered when the medical examiner performed their autopsy.

The following investigation determined that Diane was heavily intoxicated during the time of the crash. Her toxicology report showed that her blood alcohol level was at 0.19 per cent (over double the legal limit of .08 per cent), with another six grams of alcohol sitting in her stomach yet to be absorbed. Moreover, Diane had high levels of THC in her system, enough to suggest that she could have smoked marijuana as recently as fifteen minutes before the crash.

Looking at the evidence, Diane's intoxication causing the crash is the most coherent theory. Garbus's documentary put forth the theory that Diane was suffering from severe pain from a tooth abscess and may have used drugs to self-medicate. However, the autopsy did not show signs of tooth abscess. So, which is more likely? This is where Occam's Razor comes in.

Merriam-Webster describes Occam's Razor as a scientific and philosophical rule stating that entities should not be multiplied unnecessarily. This is often interpreted as the simplest competing theories

xiv How to Solve True Crime

should be preferred to the more complex ones. Often, Occam's Razor is described as the simplest explanation is usually the correct one.[6] This isn't the case, but we will discuss this in the next chapter.

If Occam's Razor is applied to this case, the most straightforward competing theory would be that Diane was drink driving. No other variables are needed to prove this theory than the evidence already presented. The proof is in the pudding; even Daniel admitted that he and Diane had consumed alcohol during the camping trip.

The case of Diane Schuler and the 2009 Taconic State Parkway crash is one where Occam's Razor is concordant. The 'razor' refers to the 'shaving away' of extraneous material and assumptions. Essentially, if it looks like a duck, walks like a duck, has feathers and quacks, it's a duck.

Let's say you are about to leave the house, but upon leaving, annoyingly, you find that your car tyre is flat. Consider the explanations: a nail stuck in the tyre wall let the air out, or someone slashed your tyre. Unless you have an enemy who will stop at nothing to inconvenience you and is prone to tyre slashing, it's more likely a nail stuck in the tyre wall.

Occam's Razor is often used as a heuristic rule of thumb for investigators within actual crime cases; if a wife dies of mysterious circumstance, and her husband suddenly comes into a significant amount of money from the life insurance policy conveniently in her name, what are we supposed to think? Occam's Razor comes from the law of parsimony, which is the idea that the theory with the fewest assumptions should be selected. Look at Diane. While there are theories about tooth abscesses, the evidence points to the theory with the fewest assumptions. Diane was driving whilst intoxicated.

But what are humans other than beings who strive to make things more complicated? Just because a theory is convenient and makes the most sense doesn't mean it is correct, and not making assumptions could be problematic.

Greats like Aristotle, Newton, Einstein, Hawking, and Sagan all bought into the law of parsimony – parsimony being defined as the 'quality of being careful with money or resources: Thrift. State of being stingy, economy in the use of a means to an end. Economy of explanation in conformity with Occam's Razor.[7] Fundamentally, these thinkers knew that the simplest explanation for a problem was preferable to a more complex one. (Usually)

This is the case with the murder of Dorothy Donovan.[8]

When Delaware factory worker Charles Holden finished an evening shift one night in June 1991, he just wanted a burger. It was around midnight in the town of Harrington; when Charles had picked up his burger, he returned to his car in the parking lot and was approached by a stranger looking for a ride.

The man said he needed to get to a hospital nearby, Georgetown, because his sister was having a baby and had been admitted. Charles was understandably hesitant but let his good nature get the better of him, and he agreed.

Charles drove the man around three miles to the junction between the highway and Kilen Pond Road before telling him that was as far as they were going. However, to his horror, the man began to attack him, attempting to assault him with Charles's screwdriver that had been lying inside the vehicle.

Fearing for his life, Charles jumped out of his car and fled towards a store for help, but the man caught up with him. He told Charles he would kill him if he did not continue the journey. Thinking fast, Charles pacified the man by relenting; he would continue the journey, and they made their way back to the car.

But, before the hitchhiker could reach the passenger side, Charles leapt into his car and sped away. Although the stranger tried to follow him and run behind the vehicle, he could not keep up, and Charles managed to leave him behind in the dust.

Charles continued his short drive home, thinking this was the end of a profoundly unpleasant encounter. To his horror, he saw the hitchhiker again as he pulled onto a street close to his property.

He drove away, made a few loops to ensure the stranger did not know where he lived, and stopped to use a nearby payphone to call the police. Myrna Kinney responded, and Charles waited for her to arrive before they went to check his property for the man.

Thankfully, Charles's house was undisturbed, but he had a sudden fearful realization. His mother, Dorothy Donovan, had a trailer almost directly behind his property and lived alone.

They found the 70-year-old lying dead in her bedroom. She had been stabbed multiple times in the face and chest. A pillow had been placed over her head. Although the window at the backdoor had been broken and was probably the entry point, there was no sign of robbery. Meaning this was not the motive.

Police were suspicious of Charles's hitchhiker story and found it hard to believe that not only should he be chased by a stranger but that his mother would also be murdered in an apparent coincidence.

The FBI was brought in and concluded that the elderly woman had probably already been known to her killer due to her home being relatively isolated.

Things somehow get even worse for Charles as the investigators discover Dorothy's life insurance policy, with him named one of the beneficiaries. Occam's Razor is about to stick a middle finger up to Charles.

With police now all but certain Charles was the murderer they were looking for – or perhaps him in collaboration with a hitman – it seemed likely that an arrest was imminent.

But then, forensics and a thorough following-up of the leads stepped in to give him a lifeline. Most tellingly, police found a bloody handprint within Dorothy's home that did not match Charles's DNA or prints. Charles was cleared, although they were still somewhat suspicious about his potential involvement. Not until fourteen years later did modern technology lead to a breakthrough. In November 2005, the DNA collected from Dorothy's home was put through the national database CODIS.

To their surprise, they got a hit.

It matched a 41-year-old man named Gilbert Cannon from Maryland, who had been living in Delaware since 1991. He was a career criminal and had served time for drug charges and robbery, resulting in his DNA being collected upon his release.[9]

By January 2006, Cannon was arrested and charged with first-degree murder. As the FBI profile suggested, he had been high on cocaine the night of the murder and looking for somewhere to sleep it off when he broke into Dorothy's property.

Curious about the strange story that led suspicion to fall so heavily on Charles, police questioned Cannon about how he came to choose that house. He confirmed that he had only gone inside Dorothy's trailer after Charles had driven away. He wandered around a little because it was the only property that was dark. He assumed it was empty and he could spend the night there, but when he found Dorothy, he killed her to make sure he could not be identified. However, he insisted that he had never seen her before.

He was as surprised as the investigators when he was informed that the woman he had killed was the mother of the man he had threatened and attacked that same evening.

Deputy Attorney General Robert O'Neill initially pursued the death penalty against Cannon, but this was eventually reduced as part of a plea deal. In April 2007, Gilbert Cannon pleaded guilty to first-degree murder and was sentenced to life in prison without the possibility of release.

There is no way of knowing if Cannon would have killed someone anyway that night in June 1991 or if his attack on Charles led indirectly to Dorothy's murder. But the case only shows that hitchhiking is better left where it belongs – within the plots of horror movies.

It also shows that while Occam's Razor is a beneficial, heuristic tool for deciding between theories, it can oversimplify a situation. It almost ruined Charles's life.

This long and convoluted introduction to Occam's Razor raises the question: can simplicity be affiliated with true crime? We must be careful with Occam's Razor lest we cut ourselves on our blades. It is essential to note what the Franciscan friar William of Ockham wanted to emphasize: that you should not complicate and not stack a theory if a more straightforward explanation was ready. Pare it down. Prune the excess.[10]

So, what better way to prune the excess than to look at confounding true crime cases, some where inane theories hold true and others where the solution is in plain sight?

In the following pages, I have put together some of my favourite, intriguing, unsettling true crime cases that defy the ordinary, or do they?

Chapter One

What is Occam's Razor, or rather, who is Occam, and what is the Razor?

Before jumping in at the deep end, we must first understand Occam's Razor.

We see elements of Occam's Razor in several different media. I first heard of Occam's Razor as a teenager, sitting at home watching CBBC's Wolfblood. Wolfblood was a quintessential teen show about teenagers who are, you guessed it, werewolves. In season one, two friends are trying to figure out if a close friend is a lycanthrope, and they utilise Occam's Razor to explain strange coincidences. They describe it as the 'simplest explanation is always right, even if it sounds crazy.'

The phrase always stuck with me: if the simplest explanation is always right, then that closes a lot of possibilities. The shadow in the corner of my room is not a wielding axe murderer but rather just a pile of clothes on my chair. However, after further research, it can be argued that Wolfblood may have interpreted Occam's Razor more generically.

Occam's Razor is often misstated as 'the simplest answer is the correct one,' whereas a more accurate explanation would be 'the simplest answer is the best starting point to investigate.' The more variables or assumptions that add up to get a solution, the more difficult it is to investigate and the less likely it is to occur.

Imagine you hear hoofbeats outside. Is that a horse or a zebra? Unless you live in an African Savanna, it will unlikely be a zebra. We would need more assumptions to prove it is a zebra. Was a zebra being imported to a local zoo, and it escaped confinement and is now wandering the streets? A horse would require one assumption: a horse is nearby. That does not mean it cannot be a zebra. It means that you should probably consider the horse first and then go from there. That shadow in the corner of my room is most likely a pile of clothes, but that does not mean it cannot be an axe murderer.

The principle of Occam's Razor has been around for centuries; however, it became more widely known after the film 'Contact' was released in 1997.[1] Based on the novel by Carl Sagan and starring Jodie Foster as a SETI scientist, it centres around the first confirmed communication received on Earth by aliens. The communication is discovered to be a diagram to build a transporter, which Foster's character uses to travel through a series of wormholes to visit the alien who made the transport possible. When Foster returns, she believes she was gone for approximately eighteen hours, but on Earth, it was like she never left. Her story was doubted, especially since the evidence she recorded was just static. She is reminded of Occam's Razor; the most possible explanation is that she never left. It is no Wolfblood, but no one can slander Jodie Foster.

The idea of Occam's Razor is frequently attributed to English Franciscan friar William of Ockham, a scholastic philosopher, apologist and Catholic theologian. He was believed to have been in Ockham, a small village in Surrey.

William took the vow of poverty very seriously and lived humbly. Something he believed the church should also have encapsulated. He was an independent thinker and rationalist, which did not go hand in hand with the church.

William said, '*pluralitas non est ponenda sine ncessitate,*' or 'plurality should not be posited without necessity.' The principle gives precedence to simplicity. You do not need to add something beyond what you believe to be true and correct.[2] He also stated that in his Summa Totius Logicae (Ockham's textbook of logic), *Frustra fit per plura quod potest fieri per pauciora.* 'It is futile to do with more things that which can be done with fewer.'[3] He was an empiricist. He believed you must experience something with your senses to know it is true. If there is no empirical evidence, then it is not valid.

Occam's Razor is beneficial because it allows us to wade through mental quagmire and make thinking more efficient. It does not mean disregarding thoughts; it is more of a guide and a rule of thumb. It tells us that because things in the universe tend to be simpler, do not make it more complex than it needs to be.

Within true crime cases, Occam's Razor eliminates elaborate theories that are hard to prove or disprove, allowing us to make conclusions with limited insight or information. You could say there needs to be concrete evidence experienced with the senses. Occam's Razor relies on our tendency to satisfy or operate within bounded rationality's confines. Since our rationality is inevitably bounded by time, mental capacity, and available information, we use Occam's Razor to make decisions that are *good enough*.

It can also be used to stop many true crime enthusiasts from glorifying cases and creating an elaborate conspiracy theory rather than seeing the victims as real people with real families and lives. They just become characters to them. Diane Schuler is a prime example because reopening the case and trying to absolve the theory that she was drink driving is almost like trying to absolve the blame and is disrespectful to the victims and survivors of the incident.

Occam's Razor allows for debunking conspiracy theories. Consider the popular conspiracy theory that Buzz Aldrin did not land on the moon because the American flag was 'waving'. People have developed elaborate theories suggesting that NASA fabricated the whole thing, but Aldrin explained that he was twisting the flagpole into the moon soil, which explains its movement. That might not be the most exciting explanation, but it is a much simpler one. Occam's Razor can help us escape the noise and focus on the basics.

Humans like focusing on the basics and simple explanations because we are lazy. Why overcomplicate things? It is how our brains are wired; our brain likes to take shortcuts. We can read as quickly as we do because the brain skips things that do not matter and completes what it knows is coming next. It is the same thing for vision; you think you see something out the corner of your eye, but you only see a vague outline; your brain knows what it expects and fills in the blanks.[4] Mental shortcuts are known as heuristics, a way for our brains to conserve energy and work more efficiently. For example, green means go.

We don't need to mention Dorothy Donovan again to prove that shortcuts are not always correct. Shortcuts can be linked to cognitive bias. Cognitive bias is a systemic error in thinking that occurs when people process information from the world around them, affecting their decisions and judgements. It is often a result of your brain's attempt at processing information. The human brain is powerful, but it can often make mistakes, sometimes based on the environment you grew up in or anything that may have influenced you. It can cause you to make a subconscious error that leads you to misinterpret information from the world around you.[5]

When a crime is committed, police investigators are often tasked with developing a subject based on evidence, but too often, their cognitive biases – unconscious beliefs they hold and inadvertent mental tendencies they have – influence this process, and it can lead to wrongful convictions. For example, Levon Brooks was wrongfully convicted of assaulting and killing his ex-girlfriend's 3-year-old daughter in Noxubee County in 1992. That same year, in a strikingly similar case, Kennedy Brewer was also accused of assaulting and killing his girlfriend's 3-year-old daughter in the same county. He was also wrongfully convicted.

Despite the apparent similarities, police and investigators homed in on Brooks and Brewer because they were the 'usual' suspects - the boyfriends. This assumption did not require more explanation. However, they did not consider all the evidence or critically evaluate all possible leads. Nearly two decades later, DNA evidence identified the person who had committed both crimes and had been an original person of interest, thankfully resulting in the exonerations of both men.

As a side note, projects such as the Innocent Project are so important. Their research has found that everyday people and law enforcement professionals are vulnerable to cognitive biases, which can lead to wrongful convictions. They advocate for reforms that prevent these convictions.

Occam's Razor is a significant tool for investigators; it's non-negotiable. But it must be wielded carefully; otherwise, the wrong people can be hurt.

Controversially, it may be considered that Occam's Razor cannot be used at all on real-world things like missing people or criminal cases. It is meant for hypothetical or conceptual situations, and even then, it is exceptionally heuristic. Can human beings with free will and their actions be boiled down to simple explanations? Oversimplifying explanations and cognitive bias can cause irreparable damage.

Yet, criminal investigations must start somewhere. Occam's Razor allows us to resist far-fetched or complex ideas, preventing us from feeling overwhelmed when we encounter a problem. It helps us break down a problem into its simplest components, making it more manageable. However, it is imperative to remember that no simple explanation is correct without corroborating evidence.

Logically, using the razor is testing multiple hypotheses and testing the one with the fewest parts first. The razor is a practical rule of thumb about applying the scientific method, not a resounding statement of probability.

When applying Occam's Razor to true crime cases, the most straightforward answer may usually be the correct one, but we need to be careful with that logic as it can backfire, and you can cut your own throat. This was the case with the homicide of Dana Laskowski.

P.S. If you want a more visual explanation of Occam's Razor, watch The Simpsons, season three, episode eight, 'Lisa's Pony.' You see Marge go through Occam's Razor.[6]

Chapter Two

The Murder of Dana Laskowski

Thirty-four miles south of Seattle sits Puyallup, Washington. Home to the Washington State Fair and the annual daffodil parade. It is the perfect slice of the South Pacific Northwest and was the home of Dana Laskowski.

On 31 August 2001, Alison Spencer and her husband anxiously waited for Dana to come and look after their children. Dana was reliable and punctual as a nanny, so it was unusual for her not to return to work without an explanation.

The Spencer's and Dana's neighbours failed to reach her, so they called the Puyallup police to request a welfare check at her home.

The police arrived at 413 Northeast Second Street at 10.37 am. They knocked on the door several times but were met with no response. They tried to find a way to peer inside; one officer checked the front window and saw a figure lying on the sofa. Was this person sleeping, having a medical emergency, or was something worse at play? Law Enforcement were called to the scene, and the police entered the home by going around the permitter, where they saw the door was partially open.

As the officers entered the house, they tried to notice if anything was out of place. They approached the figure on the sofa, seeing it was a woman with a blanket and pillow on top of her. She was lying face down. At first glance, it looked like she was sleeping. However, the fact that she had not moved or stirred with the commotion made the police believe otherwise.

As they lifted the blanket and pillow, the first thing they noticed was blood around the woman's mouth and nose. Her right arm was up so that the right side of her face rested on her right lower arm. Her body was posed grotesquely. She wore dark elasticated waist cloth pants, a tan collared t-shirt, and a gold chain. She was not wearing any underwear or socks. Her shirt was pulled up over her breasts, and her pants pulled down slightly.

Her neck, elbows and knees were bruised, and there was a one-and-a-half-inch mark on her neck that was hard to the touch. Her windpipe was cracked. All signs were pointing to foul play and homicide.

The body was Dana's.

The police were made aware that Dana Laskowski was a mother to 9-year-old triplets. To everyone's relief, her daughters were not at the crime scene. The next step in a case like this was to handle the pragmatic aspects of this case. First, Dana's family needed to be notified, and then they needed to find Dana's daughters so that they did not have to come to her home to see it marked up with caution tape, and their mother was nowhere to be found.

This is when the investigation could begin. The investigators analysed the scene and came to the following conclusions: there was no evidence of forced entry, the first-floor windows were locked, and the front door deadbolted. There was a pile of clothes next to Dana's body that was collected and placed into evidence.

There were impressions on the carpet near where Dana was discovered, making the investigators assume that her body had been dragged approximately nine inches. Police went through the home and found several open and rifled-through drawers, but they couldn't tell if anything was missing because Dana had only moved in a month prior. No one was there to identify if anything was missing; however, Dana's house keys and wallets were not accounted for.

Investigators employed the Super Glue Fuming method; the Cyanoacrylate fuming method.[1] They used vapours of super glue to develop fingerprints that can be enhanced using dyes or powders so they can be tape-lifted. Despite that, no useful fingerprints were found in Dana's house, only her own and a palm print of someone not in her direct family, but that could have been a friend of Dana's or even the triplets.

Dana was close with her family, frequently letting her 17-year-old niece Amanda stay with her. It was speculated that Amanda was troublesome, but it may be problematic because she was a *teenager*. She habitually ran away from her parent's house, seeing Dana's home as a haven where she could hang out with her friends. Dana also had a chance to watch them, often leaving her window unlocked so that Amanda or her friends could enter and shower at her house. She was a well-loved human being.

Dana's autopsy illustrated that she had bruises on her inner thigh, blood in nasal cavities, and petechiae of the eyes and face, which usually occurs during asphyxiation, when the sudden rush of blood bursts the vessels. It also revealed that Dana's murder could have been slow, with the perpetrator losing grip and trying to tighten it. Looking at the crime scene itself, the killer would have walked past a set of knives in a knife block. But they strangled her instead.

If robbery was not the primary motive, and the killer moved to strangulation (a very intimate way of murdering someone), it was more than likely it was a crime of passion. With the positioning of the body and the damage to the neck, it is evidence that the murderer had a great deal of strength.

Occam's Razor would point to a romantic interest, possibly male and someone she knew, as it seems very personal. What contradicts that theory is that there was no facial bruising. If an intimate partner was murdered and it was an act of domestic violence, the conflict may begin with arguing, escalating to attacking the face and body.

The police knew where to start the investigation, with the whereabouts of the triplets, who were with their father.

When Stan, Dana's ex-husband, was interviewed by the police, he did not hold back any information. He revealed that when he met Dana, she had been separated from her abusive husband. Nine years before Dana was murdered, they were struggling to get pregnant, so they used IVF, which gave them the triplets.

By 2001, they had been separated for a year. Stan was not near Puyallup at the time of the murder. He and the triplets were on a fishing trip at Moses Lake, which was two hours away. The last time they had spoken was on the 30th for around twenty minutes, which was an amicable conversation.

Stan had gone to the gas station before returning to the kids, he also had a receipt proving this, and then they went camping as usual. The police questioned the girls, who said their father had not left them the entire time. Stan *could* have opportunistically slipped away, but making a two-hour journey there and back without children noticing, seemed less than likely. Furthermore, the girls witnessed no violence between their parents. Stan had a solid alibi.

Next, the police spoke to the family Dana nannied for. Dana would keep a journal of the children's progress, showing what they did that day to their parents. Alison informed the police of a strange entry, 'Pat', followed by a phone number.

When Alison initially brings it up with Dana, Dana launches into a story about a man called Patrick harassing her. When she moved in, he had arrived at her home to install a cable. He was evidentially interested and asked her on a date, but she told him she was not interested in anything romantically. He didn't know how to take no for an answer; he would send flowers, poems and leave her never-ending phone calls. Dana concluded her story to Alison by omnisciently saying, 'If I ever go missing, he is the one.' Occam's Razor is positively glowing right now.

The police pulled Dana's phone records, which showed that she was only on the receiving end of these calls. She only returned a call once, on 25 July. She and Pat talked for eleven minutes.

The police actively sought out a search warrant for Pat's house, and he was brought in for questioning. Initially, he was behaving strangely. He was defiant, arrogant, and almost put out at having to be there. When they searched the house, the police found a plethora of violent letters that were focused on a woman. Patrick's behaviour did not align with his situation, so they asked him blatantly, 'Why do you think you are here?' Turns out Patrick did not read the search warrant sent to him. *Imagine not thoroughly reading the search warrant that was sent to you.*

They asked him to read it thoroughly, and he saw the words homicide and Dana, and his demeanour changed instantly. He softened, apologised for his conduct, and became more cooperative. But this does not mean he was not a suspect. He explained that the letters they found were not about Dana but about his wife, written to cope with their divorce. This may seem perfunctory, but a line in the letter did say, 'both having green eyes.' Dana's eyes were brown.

Pat confirmed that he and Dana never dated, but he was interested in her. On the day of her murder, he was at work all day, and he did not hesitate to provide fingerprints and DNA for testing. He also revealed a fascinating titbit of information: Dana was romantically involved with a man called Mike from Canada. Chasing this lead, detectives tracked Mike down.

Mike lived in Canada and was an avid filmmaker. Due to the short distance between them, Mike and Dana would spend weekends together. On 28 August, he spent the night with Dana at her house, got up at 4.00 am, and drove back to Canada.

The last time they spoke was via the phone on 30 August, when they talked for seven minutes. Mike tried to call again, but Dana didn't answer the phone.

Concerned, Mike drove to Washington to see if everything was alright, but he was stopped at the border and given a ticket for having a suspended licence. The ticket was proof and alibi enough. Learning of Dana's murder from Alison, Mike was helpful and provided DNA willingly.

Six weeks before her murder, Dana and her friend Shauna went to a festival with their friend John. They wanted to keep the fun going and went to a bar afterwards for a few more drinks. However, Dana ended up going home with John.

John brought Dana back to where she and Shauna were staying, where he told her that he and Dana had sex. This threw a spanner in the works, remember Mike? Mike and John were best friends.

When Dana talked to Shauna, she told her that Mike would 'flip out' on her if he found out. In fact, the last words she said were, 'If I end up dead, you know who did it.'

We can infer here that John wanted to be with Dana, and so did Mike. Did Mike suspect what was going on, and would that give him a motive? Would jealousy influence John and motivate him? If you were to incorporate Occam's Razor, jealousy between Mike and John, causing one of them to murder her, could be the explanation with the fewest assumptions. Crimes of passion are often fuelled by jealousy like this. It would not be too implausible. If you look at the crime scene, the murder was not meticulously done. It was in the heat of an an altercation and confrontation. Dana was also covered with a blanket. Could this show that the person who killed her knew her? Is it offering a level of care?

John was a new thread that investigators wanted to pull on. When they talked to John, he revealed that a few days after he and Dana slept together, she called and asked if he would tell Mike the truth. He said he would not lie about it if Mike brought it up. A few days passed, and Dana called John again, asking if John was going to a festival in Vancouver and whether they could go together. John said yes but refused to go with Dana unless she came clean with Mike. Dana said she did not want to go to the festival at all. She wanted to see John, but not if it rocks the boat with Mike.

Detectives pressed John about his whereabouts on the day of Dana's murder; he was at home alone until 4.30 pm, and later that afternoon, he was running errands with friends. He swung by Mike's place, who, at this point, was panicking due to Dana's lack of response. The Police were able to verify John's account of events.

What is concerning is that John did not come clean about the affair with Mike till the end of September, which is suspicious, to say the least. Surely, you would try to absolve yourself in case something came out and was misconstrued. Mike was furious when he found out and kicked John out of the house, but there was no violent interaction. Nothing out of the ordinary.

Fast forward to early 2002, and the suspects were drying up. This case is unique because there have been so many potential suspects, but they were all fruitless.

Dana's family have been waiting so long for some sort of absolution and closure, and in desperation, the investigators went to the FBI for advice. Who blatantly said they did not think it was Stan. Even though Stan had a life insurance policy in Dana's name, making him a prime suspect, they attested that if he wanted to make use of the insurance policy, he would make sure he would have had a foolproof method to murder Dana. Or even if it was a crime of passion, there would be bruises on Dana's face from an emotional altercation. Stan was technically ruled out.

The FBI has the idea to check the guestbook where Dana's crypt was kept, where those who visited could have a place to vent their grief.

When the investigators flipped through the book, they saw many entries from Mike and quite a few from Amanda. One of Amanda's that caught their eye was 'thirty-seven days sober, all for you. I wish I was a better niece to you.' Is this an admission of guilt? The FBI said this was a valid avenue to explore as it seemed remorseful.

The police questioned Amanda again, who mentioned the 'troubled' group of friends she hung out with. All these friends knew Dana and would frequent her house as the place to hang out and be themselves. Dana and Amanda even ventured into recreational drugs together (marijuana). They asked if she knew of anyone who may have been strong enough to kill Dana, and she pointed to a friend named Blaine, who she alleged attacked her after she rejected him. She also recalled seeing Blaine with scratches on his arms following Dana's death. A guilty reaction?

They learned that Blaine had a violent criminal history, including weapons and drug-related charges. However, when the police could not extradite Blaine from a different state, they reached out to someone in prison who knew their suspect and made a disquieting claim. It was not Blaine who killed Dana, but Emily Lauenborg, Amanda's best friend.

Two other people in Amanda's friend group soon echoed these allegations; it was Emily, who was abnormally strong for her size, who had killed Dana, and everyone knew it.

Emily's criminal record began in 1997 when she was caught shoplifting, which is not atypical for this age group; it is a harmless experimentation of mortality, which is fine. Yet in 1998, the delinquent behaviour escalated when Emily stole money from her teacher's purse. She denied it when confronted, but then she confided in a friend and was soon arrested.

In January 2001, Emily was arrested again for first-degree theft for stealing jewellery and cufflinks to pawn the items for cash. Emily went to rehab during the months following Dana's murder.[2]

When called into questioning, Emily angrily denied having killed Dana but was not able to provide investigators with an alibi for the night of the murder.

When the police searched Emily's home, they found a diary with an incriminating list of things Emily wanted to do before she died, like a bucket hit list. As part of that entry, Emily wrote that she wanted to 'kill someone and get away with it.'

In another entry, Emily talked about her anger at Amanda and wrote about strangling her 'just like her aunt.' The final nail in the coffin the police found in the search was a t-shirt Emily wore to Dana's funeral. It was Dana's T-shirt.

After the search, Amanda cooperated with the investigation and finally revealed what happened to her aunt. On the night of Dana's murder, after using drugs, Amanda and Emily had gone to her house in search of money to buy more drugs. Emily and Dana got into a fight, and when Dana asked Emily to leave, Emily started choking her. Amanda did not get involved in the fight and attempted to block it out. That is when she said she heard a crack and a gurgle. Dana died. The two robbed her and left.

Regarding motive, authorities speculated that Emily was jealous of Dana's influence on Amanda and wanted her out of her best friend's life. It was crucial information authorities needed, but the prosecutors doubted that they could prove Emily's guilt to a jury due to her inconspicuous physical size and instead let her plead guilty to the lesser charge of manslaughter. She was found guilty and sentenced to six and a half years in prison.

Meanwhile, Amanda escaped charges in exchange for her testimony.

While Dana's family was relieved to have some type of justice served and some sort of closure, they were disappointed with how little time Emily served after killing Dana. She changed her name, moved away from Washington, married, and had children.[3]

This case is discombobulating, to say the least. I have never seen a case with so many suspects, but they were all inefficacious. Bring Occam's Razor into it, and we can say the case sticks a finger up at it. If Occam's Razor were to work in this case and refers to the theory that makes the fewest assumptions, then it would have been either Stan or Patrick. The homicide of Dana Laskowski is a prime example of how simple explanations within true crime may be a good starting point for investigation, but they are not always practical. Occam's Razor did not lead us to the answer in the case, but no one guessed the correct answer either, or if anyone did, it was probably based on evidence and not because they were good at wild guesses.

Chapter Three

The Murder of Jane Britton

In the colder months, the grounds of Harvard University became a palette of browns, greys and whites. Leafless trees heavy with morning frost, the cement paved a ribbon through frostbitten grass. This idyllic landscape served as a backdrop for thousands of anxious students preparing for their examinations.

On the evening of 6 January 1969, the first Monday of the new year and day classes resumed after the holiday break, 23-year-old Jane Britton joined other anthropology classmates for dinner at a local restaurant. After this, she and her boyfriend, James Humphries, went ice skating on the Common. James returned with Jane to her apartment complex on University Avenue at 10.30 pm. The building sat just outside Harvard Square to the west, not far from the Charles River. He left her for the evening at 11.30 pm. Around midnight, Jane went to her neighbours, the Mitchells, for some sherry.

The following day, the snow had melted into a soup of grey slush as frigid temperatures were replaced by a slightly warmer atmosphere. The anthropology students gathered to take their examinations, one last hurdle they needed to jump before undertaking their doctoral thesis; one student was missing, however. Jane.

Jane was known as a lively student with dark, straight hair that framed her face. It was customary for her to appear in the student lobby after brief periods of absence. Despite the bouts of isolation, she was chatty and personable. Jane was a model student, joining the PhD programme straight out of Radcliffe College. Her parents, a Radcliffe College Vice President and a medieval history scholar raised her to take her education seriously. She graduated Magna Cum Laude from Radcliffe College in 1967.

At Harvard, she served as a teaching assistant and helped uncover the remains of a Neolithic Community during an archaeological dig in Iran.

Her favourite quote is from Vonnegut's *The Sirens of Titan*; 'I was the victim of a series of accidents, as are we all.'[1]

In short, she was exemplary and dedicated academically. So missing the exam was peculiar.

James Humphries called her after taking the exam himself, but the phone rang endlessly. His knocks went unanswered on Jane's gold-painted apartment door, so he tried the handle, which was unlocked. This was not unusual because Jane and the Mitchells shared a fridge, so the door was usually unlocked for easy access. And the building was not known for its safety, but more on that later.

Humphries' knocking was loud enough to draw the attention of Donald Mitchell, a fellow anthropology student, and the two men decided to enter the unlocked residence.

When he walked into the apartment, James noted the kitchen window was wide open, the January air seeped into the space, books and manuscripts were draped haphazardly on the floor, intertwined with ashtrays. It's when James stepped further into the apartment that he found her.

Jane was lying face down on her bed, a leg dangling off the side of the mattress, her blue nightgown pulled up to her waist, her body partially obscured by blankets and a fur coat. Thinking she was sick and due to her slightly compromising position, he went next door and asked Jill Mitchell if she could look closer. When she did, she discovered Jane's head was caked with blood. She removed all the items covering Jane, uncovering blood *everywhere*. On the pillow, the sheet, clotted and flaking at the back of Jane's neck. They promptly called the Cambridge police, who, upon arrival, asked medical examiner Dr Arthur McGovern to come to Britton's apartment as well. McGovern soon confirmed the worst; Jane was dead.

Three Cambridge police officers were called to the apartment to collect evidence, weaving their way through the hallways. The officers noted the open kitchen window and noticed something stranger; nothing in the apartment had been stolen. Many valuable items such as money, jewellery and artefacts were strewn about the ground, but nothing had been touched.

Detectives gingerly stepped around to see if the intruder would have any motive or had forced an entry, to no indication. The only proof that anything terrible had happened was Jane herself.

Whilst one detective stayed behind to scope for evidence and fingerprints, the other two began speaking to other tenants to see if anything unusual had happened. They received the same message; nothing strange had occurred the night before.

Jane's medical examiner, Dr George Katsas, had performed the autopsy at Watson Funeral Home. He found multiple lacerations to the head with underlying skull fractures, cracking her skull. The coroner also noticed a bruise on her arm and two shallow gashes on her forehead, suggesting that she was facing her attacker when she was initially attacked.

They ruled the death a homicide by blunt force trauma that had occurred roughly ten hours before the body was discovered, but the detectives did not find any sort of weapon at the scene.

From the shape of the head wounds, the murder weapon had a point, but the investigators could not determine precisely what had been used. 'It was something sharp, like a hatchet or cleaver', stated Leo Davenport, the lead detective on the case.

Back at the Cambridge police station, what had begun as a typical average day had been worked up into a frenzy of activity. Leo Davenport wasted no time. Jane's parents, Ruth and J.Boyd Britton, were the first to be interviewed. Her father was a relatively well-known person in Cambridge; he was a public figure, but his wife Ruth was not. And the news of her daughter's death was justifiably too much to bear.

Ruth had spoken to Jane on the phone on Monday night. Jane had been worried about her exams, but that was all. At no point was Jane acting strangely; the parents' statements did not shed any light on why Jane may have been murdered, so the police had to continue their investigation.

Leo Davenport knew James Humphries would be the next port of call to interview and called him in shortly after Jane's parents left. He stayed in the interrogation room for hours, answering any question that Davenport had for him. Still, just like Jane's parents, his testimony did not provide any insight into the aberrant nature of Jane's death.

Around midnight, Davenport had gathered the media and press, eagerly waiting outside the station, into the conference room to make his position known and clear up any brewing rumours.

The detective knew he would need their cooperation in this investigation. He confirmed they had no suspects at that point but with the evidence they had gathered at the crime scene, they determined that there was no forced entry and no sign of struggle, so they were under the impression that she knew the person who killed her.

The building itself was no stranger to violent acts against women. In 1963, Beverly F. Samans was found dead at least two days before her body was discovered in her first-floor apartment at 4 University Road. She had been strangled with a stocking. Her hands were tied behind her back with another stocking, and puncture wounds covering her body, leading police to believe she may have been tortured before she was slain.

It was the ninth strangling to take place in the Metropolitan Boston area within 11 months.[2]

So, the press wanted to know if this attack was associated with the previous attacks, but Davenport denied that there was a connection based on the crime scene. They confirmed that she was murdered with a blunt object with a pointed end, and the assailant struck her from all sides of the head, sometimes with extreme force, cracking her skull. The coroner also acknowledged two gashes in her forehead, suggesting that she was facing her attacker when she was initially attacked.

While Leo Davenport gave his statement, inside the building on 6 University Road, the tenants were incapable of rest, no one felt safe going to sleep that night, and a lot of the tenants were single women who gathered that night hoping that strength in numbers would save them from the same fate. The killer was still out there, and they could kill again.

Jane Britton had only been dead for a day, but by 8 January 1969, the story of her death was on the front page of every newspaper in Boston. Even the *New York Post* could not resist publishing a story.

Reporters roamed the campus, searching for people who may know something about Jane or her death.

Leo Davenport was obligated to inform the press about their findings and investigation. At his next briefing, he reported the following: whilst they had no suspects, there were two leads they were going to follow. One was Jane's ex-boyfriend, who had recently dropped out of the anthropology department and was spotted around Cambridge in the last few weeks. And the second is a man who allegedly had his romantic advances rejected by Jane. They did not disclose the names at the time, and they also revealed that they were still looking for the murder weapon. A potential weapon of choice had gone missing from the archaeology department. It was a stone, six inches in length, with a sharp pointed end.

The rumour mill was running with the anthropology students; people were particularly interested in the second man Davenport talked about. The one whom Jane rejected just before her death. Some students insinuated that it might be a professor in the anthropology department, someone called Professor Karl Lamberg-Karlovsky. Most of the professors in the anthropology department had conservative views. To say the least, to say the most, they were misogynists. Female students were barely tolerated. The cultural gap between the students and the professors was enlarging. They hired a younger professor to bridge this gap, so he was somewhat culturally closer to the students.

Karlovsky joined the Harvard Anthropology Department in 1965 when he was 28. His appearance was in stark contrast to his tweed-wearing colleagues. He was known to wear leather jackets and pull up to class on his motorbike.

Other students felt that Jane could have been killed by a random person as Cambridge was not the safest place. Contemporary newspaper accounts describe the building as decrepit and unsafe. The *New York Times* called it "seedy and roach-infested" with peeling paint in the hallways.[3]

The *Harvard Crimson* reported that the "littered and dingy" building had no locks on the outside doors, despite repeated pleas from tenants to install them along with a buzzer system to further restrict entry to their guests. Jane's apartment door had a lock so dysfunctional she rarely used it; the Mitchells said she intended to move out of the building early the following year.[4]

Friends of Jane recalled that while an undergraduate at Radcliffe, she had fought off an attacker on the Common with a penknife, slashing his clothes in the process; the incident had not been reported to the police.[5]

Despite keeping them up to date, the reporters were hungry for more information, and Davenport had left them starving.

After only an extra day of investigating, officers called reporters again for a conference to update them. This is where they revealed that after canvassing the crime scene, they realised that Jane's body, along with the floor, walls, and ceiling, had been sprinkled with a reddish-brown powder identified as either red ochre or iron oxide. They revealed to the press that ancient Iranians and many other cultures spread it over the dead as a funeral rite. So, the murder may have been committed by someone who knew of the cultural significance of this powder. The press went into a frenzy at this reveal, newspaper stories spreading like wildfire stating that Jane's death was part of a ritualistic killing.

For some, this information brought some relief. It was believed that Jane could not have been killed by a random person as the details and the killing were too specific. It was a welcome consolation for students worried they could be next. But their fears had heightened for anthropology students as the presence of red ochre meant it could have been one of them. Especially when they realised that one of the only people in the department who had access to red ochre was Karlovsky. Occam's Razor would say Karlovsky was the ultimate culprit.

But, at this point, rumours were the only tangible evidence of Karlovsky killing Jane. Rumours are about as tangible as candyfloss. Nevertheless, the police were grasping at straws, and Karlovsky made a compelling suspect. The professor, who had claimed to have discovered Alexander the Great's Lost citadel, was pompous and imposing. He sometimes roamed the halls in a cape. He was also Jane's faculty adviser at the time of her death. There was known to be aversive tension between the two; he had failed her on the school's general exams and warned her that her career could be in trouble if she did not pass the next time.

In 1968, just six months before her death, Jane went on a dig in Iran with Karlovsky, joined by James and a handful of others, during which the professor disparaged her work but allegedly took an interest in Jane. Presumably, the married Karlovsky was not against pursuing female students, but he was up for tenure now that Jane had died. Did he abuse his power to get her into bed? Did he only promise a good grade in exchange for sexual favours?

When interviewed by the press, Karlovsky was adamant that any rumours that he and Jane had an inappropriate relationship could be disparaged. He also did not believe that Jane's murder was a ritualistic killing. He didn't think that just because the body was covered in red ochre, it had anything to do with a Middle Eastern ritual. He told the detectives the same thing, stating that red ochre was a ubiquitous substance that could be purchased at any art store. He wanted to discount any ideas that Jane's death was sacrificial. Red ochre is a pigment, and it was used in ancient civilizations for all sorts of things, but it is also used now in paint dyes. Karlovsky explained that Jane may have had the red ochre as she painted or used it to dye fabric. He was right. Jane was a painter in her spare time. She had covered an entire wall with a mural of cats, giraffes and owls in swirling, dreamy colours.

The professor had made a valid point. The police, like much of Cambridge, had been so caught up in the possibility of a ritualistic killing that they had not spent much time looking for other explanations. Occam's Razor would have been utilised to look at the evidence presented, the red ochre and the fact that the teacher who would have had access to it was rumoured to not have the most amicable relationship with Jane. However, Occam's Razor also says the most straightforward answer is the best starting point to investigate, not the only point.

The detectives had been hoping that the sample of red ochre from Karlovsky might prove something special about the substance, such as a specific kind of iron oxide that could connect Jane's death with some ancient ritual significance. However, analysing the sample did not bring forth any information. After several calls to local art supply stores, the professor was right that red ochre was common in art supplies. And Jane was a painter in her spare time, so the clues were all there. Ritualistic sacrifice may have been a great way to sell papers, but it did not make it accurate.

Unfortunately, the idea of a ritual killing was so scandalous and shocking that it was easy to get carried away, which is precisely what the public, the press and the police had done. The red ochre was the primary link between Jane and the professor, but now that connection was broken.

Davenport was getting desperate. They had been distracted by a red herring, so they needed a new lead fast.

The press thought the same thing. With the theory of the red ochre going south, the reporters clamoured in to fill the space with new developments. The newest scope? The slowness of the investigation.

It became increasingly apparent that the police had no idea who killed Jane and the press was happy to latch onto those failings. The Cambridge police had a reputation for cooperating with the press, with detectives gladly working alongside reporters and offering them information when it was safe. Even the chief of police was known to be friendly with the press, but this new angle put pressure on that relationship.

Late on the afternoon of 10 January, Chief James Reagan said that from then on, detectives would need his permission to disclose any information about the case. He claimed that this was due to inaccuracies in reporting on the case. It was a media blackout.[6]

Media blackouts are fraught with ethical challenges. Journalists have a responsibility to report the news. Indeed, information-sharing is one of the most basic principles of journalism. But news organizations are also dedicated to minimizing harm: they must ensure the words they publish will not endanger another person's life. They could be risking Karlovsky's life by focusing on a rumour, but now they can't help the public by feeding them information that can make sure they take the necessary precautions to stay safe.

Going back into the case, the police were still unsure if Jane had been sexually assaulted, and they would not know until they received the chemical analysis report. The police sent several samples for inspection, all taken from Jane's apartment. A blood-stained pillow, a pair of jeans, underwear and a candelabra that had flecks of dried blood around its handle. The detectives did not have to wait long. Soon, Detective Leo Davenport got the call.

The chemist explained that the blood samples from the crime scene were all type O blood and were all from one person, Jane. But someone else, potentially the killer, had left his DNA through another method. Jane's underwear and her pillow tested positive for semen. This could mean that there had been sexual activity before Jane's death.

The chemists also analysed the contents of Jane's stomach and found another helpful detail. There was alcohol in her system, and it had not given enough time to metabolize and enter her bloodstream before she died slowly. This was the sherry from the night before.

Further interviews with Jane's friends and family would reveal that Jane did not like entertaining guests in her nightgown, and her boyfriend had already left for the evening. So, she was not expecting company and did not know her attacker. And if that is the case, she may have been raped before she was killed. DNA tracing was not nearly as advanced as it is now, and frankly, it did not exist. There was no such thing as a DNA database and no way to identify someone through their DNA. There was no way to trace the semen found in Jane's apartment. The toxicology report had been helpful but hardly enough to make a break in the case.

Now, everyone was a suspect in this case. This is Occam's Razor's worst nightmare.

Davenport re-interviewed Jane's friends and neighbours, hoping someone might have heard or seen something on that fateful night. Canvassing the building did, however, produce a few leads. A child in another apartment in the building recalled hearing unusual noises on the fire escape that night. Another neighbour of Britton's told police that he had seen a man whom he described as about 6 feet (180 cm) tall and 170 pounds (77 kg) running away from the building at 1.30 am.

But the more information the investigators had gathered, the less valuable it became. How are they expected to chase ghosts and fragments?

While the investigation became a quagmire of unhelpful information, Mr and Mrs Britton buried their daughter.

The funeral occurred thirty minutes outside Cambridge in a plain grey stone church near Jane's childhood home. Still, no distance could keep away curious onlookers who wanted to follow the mystery of the murdered student. The Cambridge police nonetheless filmed her funeral service, in case someone in attendance had been involved and gave themselves away by their behaviour, to no avail. A growing congregation of people would come to ogle at the morbid affair. In the church, mourners in crowded pews were surrounded by reporters and policemen, and a shared room was packed with people jostling for space and craning their necks to catch a glimpse of the casket. Jane's parents and brother sat in front of the church; their emotions were concealed from nosy spectators as many curious eyes glanced towards them. There was no eulogy or other statements from Jane's family or friends, and the service lasted only thirty minutes.

As time ticked, it was harder for the police to get reliable statements from anyone. Jane's neighbours struggled to remember everything from a month ago, and the case had gone cold. And the Britton family was beginning to give up hope on finding any closure of who killed their beloved daughter. Harvard University was more than happy to move on from this scandal. It seemed even the police had forgotten about Jane Britton as other cases began taking up Leo Davenport's time, and without the proper technology to analyse the semen found in Jane's apartment, there was no use chasing a ghost. The killer was out there, but no one was looking for him.

The police would have to wait more than a decade for science to meet their needs. In the mid-1980s, a new form of criminal analysis was made available to the public: genetic fingerprinting. A method of DNA analysis that could identify someone from their skin cells, hair, and bodily fluids. Soon, genetic fingerprinting became standard for criminal negotiations. This was just the thing that Jane Britton's investigators needed; her murder had gone unsolved for over a decade, but it had never been officially closed.

The samples from the investigation were still intact and could be tested using this method. Still, it is one thing to identify many components of a DNA sample, and it is entirely different to match the sample to something specific.

At this point in the case, the investigation had turned away from the theory that Jane knew her killer, so when the police tested the DNA sample from the crime scene. They ran it against the newly formed DNA criminal database. Genetic fingerprinting was a new method in the 1980s, and there had not been much time to build up a robust pool of samples. So, Jane Britton's case samples were meaningless without a large selection of DNA profiles.

The investigation had to wait.

As the decades passed, the Jane Britton case became a ghost story in Cambridge, Massachusetts. Harvard students frightened each other with the unsolved mystery of the young woman found beaten to death in her apartment.

Fast forward to 2009. As true crime became popular with documentaries and books, online forums began sprouting up for people fascinated by mysteries, and it was only a matter of time before someone brought up the murder of Jane Britton. In comes Becky Cooper.

Becky Cooper wrote the book *We Keep the Dead Close*,[7] diving into Jane's true crime narrative. She explains how, in the early 2010s, a small group of people began speculating about Jane's death. The detectives might have overlooked the investigation and potential leads on boards online. If the police could not solve the case, maybe this group could look at the case files and see something they missed.

When Becky first heard of the case, she was told about the whispered secret that made the rounds at Harvard for decades. In 1969, a professor (presumably Karlovsky) beat his student to death in her university apartment, then sprinkled red ochre dust on her body in a macabre post-mortem ritual. The motive, Cooper was told, involved a lover's quarrel. The suspect had seduced his victim, 23-year-old Jane Britton, then killed her to keep their affair hidden.

But the professor was never charged, and he continued to teach at Harvard all this time later, a tenured faculty member in the university's elite anthropology department.

Becky Cooper and Alyssa Bertetto – moderator of the Unresolved Mysteries subreddit- began looking into the case and tried to access copies of investigatory records. Becky found in her research on Jane's case that the files had been transferred from the Cambridge Police Department to the Middlesex County District Attorney's office.

Most of these access requests were denied.

When the journalists did receive records, they were constrained, sometimes just consisting of newspaper clippings of articles about the case. Even the documents that had been shared with the authors of those articles were withheld. This was a typical pattern for law enforcement in Massachusetts to refuse to release all but the most basic information about long-cold cases.

Becky and Alyssa filed lawsuits against the city of Cambridge to force the release of the case files, arguing that fresh leads had been generated by releasing information from long-cold cases in other jurisdictions.

During preparations for the court hearings in the cases, police and prosecutors reviewed all the information they had. While doing so, they looked at the DNA evidence again and considered whether it was time to have it processed again in the hope of finding a match. The state police told them newer forensic techniques could process more of the DNA, making it more likely that they could find a match this time. The investigators decided to try again.

The 2017 DNA analysis was able to recover enough DNA to run through a sex offender database, and it got a match.

It was a soft hit, which meant that police still needed to confirm the match through other tests, but they had a name: Michael Sumpter. The police got to work and discovered valuable clues.

Michael Sumpter was from Boston. He had a girlfriend in Cambridge during the 1960s. In 1967, two years before Jane's death, he worked less than a mile from her apartment.

He was a serial rapist whose name had been added to the national sex offender register shortly after he was convicted of sexual assault in 1975 and was sent to prison for the first time. Finally, the investigation had a lead suspect. The forensic test was inconclusive, and the police would have to gather more samples from Sumpter to compare.

There was just one problem. Michael Sumpter was dead. He passed away in 2001.

Instead, they would have to find another male directly related to Michael Sumpter. That person would have the same unique pattern of Y chromosomes that had allowed the crime lab to identify Michael Sumpter as a genetic match to find a suitable one. So, they turned to an unexpected place: a genealogy website. Ancestry.com.[8]

On Ancestry.com, the investigators found Sumpter's brother, who provided them with a sample. This sample matched the one believed to be his brother closely enough to eliminate all but 0.08% of the human male population as suspects.

During Sumpter's lifetime, he was convicted of two rapes, the second of which occurred when he escaped from a work release program while he was serving his sentence for the first. Earlier investigations had found similar matches between his DNA and that of two others previously unsolved Cambridge rape-murders in the early 1970s, predating his first conviction, as well as another unsolved rape, bringing his lifetime total of known offences to five rapes and three murders.

At a November 2018 news conference, Middlesex County District Attorney Marian T. Ryan announced the results of the investigation: 'Michael Sumpter…has been identified as the person responsible for the 1969 murder of Jane Britton.' Although Sumpter could not be tried due to his death, Marian stated, 'I am confident that the mystery of who killed Jane Britton has finally been resolved and the case is officially closed.'[9]

Forty-nine years after her murder, Jane's killer had finally been found.

The exact details of Jane Britton's death were still unclear.

But her apartment building was known to be unsafe, with deadbolts that never worked and easy window access from the fire escape. It would have been relatively simple for Michael Sumpter to sneak in unnoticed during late-night hours. Jane was likely asleep when he entered her apartment. No murder weapon was ever discovered, but it is possible that Sumpter attacked her physically at first, hitting her head repeatedly with something.

So she would not be able to fight back.

Then, he raped her.

It is still unknown when or why Michael Sumpter covered Jane's upper half with rugs and coats. It could have been to stifle her screams or as a way of hiding the bloody carnage of her beaten head. It may have been so he did not have to see what she looked like, almost out of guilt.

It was unclear how the red ochre spilt across the crime scene, but some speculate that it was kicked up from Jane's room during the struggle. However, regardless of his intentions, Michael Sumpter likely left as he arrived undetected out the window before running off through the wet January night in the dark.

The discovery of Jane Britton's killer was both a relief and a disappointment. It took decades for the police to close the case. By that point, Jane had been dead for nearly fifty years. Her parents had passed away, and many of her friends had moved on.

It is bittersweet. Her investigation was plagued by red herrings. The police and the public wanted to imagine that her death was a ritualistic sacrifice. Still, at the end of the day, she was killed by an opportunistic stranger, and her murder was only one in a series of his violent crimes.

Could we say Occam's Razor worked here? I suppose it depends on which theory you find 'simplest', the idea that a professor killed her to hide a disreputable relationship that was never proven, or the opportunistic stranger looking for his next victim? It depends on how it is implemented. At the end of the day, Occam's Razor asks that you use it as a rule of thumb, start with the simplest explanation with the evidence pointed towards it, and expand, one way or the other, it helps you trim away the excess.

If the technology has been there, this case may have been solved quickly and efficiently. Cases such as these tend to get drowned in wild speculation and bizarre theories, such as the red ochre. However, this was not the case. Jane was not killed by a person with a theme. It was all just a coincidence.

Jane Britton's apartment at 6 University Road has been updated and renovated. Its successor a few blocks away is called The Craigie Arms. The structure has the same red brick with rounded columns dotted with windows. The apartments themselves have hardwood floors and arched doorways, which have been disconnected from the history of the original building. Jane's apartment is long gone. Her murals have been covered up, the wallpaper is not peeling off the walls, and the locks on the doors work, perhaps unsurprisingly.

Unfortunately, Jane Britton is not mentioned on The Craigie Arm's website, and traces of Jane amongst the student body are just fragments of different ghost stories.

Chapter Four

The Murder of Juliana Redding

C ourt cases can be so calamitous, each side fighting to tell their version of the truth rather than the correct one. In a case like this, with so much evidence, it almost seemed like the defence was working to exonerate a guilty person. This is the case with the murder of Juliana Redding, and it can be argued that her killer was allowed to walk away free.

On 16 March 2008, just after 6.00 pm, Officer Scott McGowen arrived at the Santa Monica, California home of Juliana Redding. He was responding to a welfare check made by Juliana's mother in Arizona after several failed attempts to reach her by phone.[1]

McGowan's knocking and shouting went unanswered. He checked the door handle, and the front door was locked. He walked around the property for good measure, thinking Juliana might just be out with friends. But that is when he notices the pungent smell of gas and a spot of blood on the sidewalk. He radios in for backup. Law enforcement and the fire department manage to pick the apartment locks when they are smacked in the face with the acrid smell of gas.

The police notice a burning candle on the coffee table. They moved into the apartment into the kitchen, where one of the stove's burners was turned up with the pilot light off.

This was a bomb waiting to go off, and it probably would have levelled the entire building. *A fast way to get rid of the evidence.*

But the police were lucky. It was an old house, and the gas did not concentrate enough to explode. Both were put out immediately. From the kitchen, McGowen had a view into Juliana's bedroom, where she lay on her bed.

She could have been sleeping, but the tracks on the floor indicated otherwise. The tracks indicated that she had been dragged into her bedroom by arms or legs. All over her body were signs of trauma and a struggle, not just all over her body but all over the apartment.

Who was Juliana Maureen Redding? 21-year-old Juliana was a striking young woman, destined for big things. When she walked into a room, people naturally gravitated towards her. She had a magnetic personality. She was an aspiring model and actress with a love for academia.[2]

In 2005, at nineteen years old, Juliana moved to Los Angeles to pursue her dream of acting and modelling. She started off on sound footing, landing a small role in an independent film, *Kathy T,* filmed in Atlanta. In addition to the film, she landed other small jobs, a lingerie shoot, and a few music videos. These roles would equate to nearly $3000 each.

Juliana lived in the trendy oceanfront city of Santa Monica. In late 2007, she found a quaint apartment in a complex surrounded by a white picket fence on the 1500 block of Centinela Avenue. It was a block off Santa Monica Boulevard and within easy distance of Beverly Hills and Sunset Boulevard hotspots. Like many other dwellings, Juliana's apartment had a high-security door and bars on its windows. It seemed safe enough; the complex was entirely composed of single-level units, making the bars and the security doors seem like a good idea.

As well as modelling and acting, Juliana aspired to be an academic. She was studying at Monica College and used her job as a restaurant hostess to pay for her tuition. She was known to lead with her academia rather than her beauty. Juliana also had a taste for the good life, as is her right. Her confidant, Genevieve Stewart, whom she met at Santa Monica College where they were both full-time students, said that 'she lived a pretty fancy lifestyle, she was a jet setter, she liked to travel, she liked to do fun things.'

In early 2008, Julianna got a break when she was featured in a pictorial in Maxim magazine's "Hometown Hotties" feature.[3] This success was short-lived.

From the kitchen, McGowan could see Redding's body on the bed in the bedroom. The deep purple discolouration on the bottom of her feet and the back of her thighs was a sign that the heart had stopped pumping hours earlier and the blood had begun to pool. He knew she was dead.

The investigation began straight away. With the high security of the departments and the fact there was no forced entry, Juliana either must have known her attacker or she did not expect hostile intent.

Crime scene investigators collected a large amount of DNA at the crime scene. Blood was found on Juliana's skin, clothes, mobile phone, and the stove knob. Blood drops were on a plate.

'I can tell you in eighteen years of prosecuting cases, I've never had this much DNA,' former Los Angeles County prosecutor Alan Jackson (the original prosecutor on this case) stated. 'The DNA on that stove knob, which you'd expect because someone turned it on. DNA on the front and back of Juliana's t-shirt and possibly, most importantly, DNA on her throat.'[4]

As well as Juliana's DNA, there was plenty of other DNA, maybe from the assailant, all over the crime scene. With this information, police sent those DNA samples to the lab. Meanwhile, they built a timeline.

A neighbour had reported hearing screams and furniture being moved around 9.53 pm. Another telling clue was found in Juliana's mobile phone. Jackson stated that 'when Juliana's phone was recovered, the evidence very clearly shows that 911 was dialled and the call was terminated before it could go through.' She had been calling the police for help when the killer snatched the phone from her hands and hung up. The call for help from Redding's mobile phone was attempted at 9.52 p.m. the night before her body was found. Investigators estimated she died shortly after the call.

The murder did not happen quickly. The dispute took place throughout the whole apartment. Jackson described it as a 'fight to the death.'

A forensic pathologist who performed the autopsy on Juliana recounted the contusions and cuts that covered her body. Police believed that the killer entered Juliana's apartment just before 10.00 pm. They smashed Juliana's head against the floor, causing deep contusions in her skull. She had burst capillaries in her eyes, indicating that the killer had clenched Juliana's throat so tightly that the flow of blood stopped. The bones in her neck had been crushed. There were scratches underneath her chin, coming from her fingernails, as Juliana fought desperately to break her attacker's grip.

Jackson said, 'That is the natural reaction, and that's an extremely common injury that we see [...] you immediately grab for your own throat, and Juliana did that in this case.' She broke fingernails, and things around the house were shattered and broken. The injury to Julianna's head showed that her attacker repeatedly smashed her head against the floor while they were choking her. It is indicative of just how hard she fought to live.

Although police did not divulge the precise location where they found her body, it was clear to them that her death was the result of a homicide.

Lt. Alex Padilla, the spokesman for the Santa Monica Police Department, told ABC News. 'At that point, we started interviewing neighbours about who'd seen her last. Now we're trying to put the pieces together.'[5]

Because of the ongoing investigation, Padilla did not reveal if anything was missing from Redding's apartment. Although the information that was initially revealed by the SMPD to ABC News indicated that Redding had 'died as a result of an assault,' Padilla declined to provide details surrounding the nature of the physical attack and would not say whether a weapon had been used. Following protocol, investigators decided early on that they would do everything possible to preserve the investigation's integrity and avoid compromising comments.

That didn't stop media accounts from America's Most Wanted, AOL News and CNN from releasing reports that the cause of death was blunt force trauma. These reports were refuted by the Los Angeles County Coroner's Office.

'Those media reports are not accurate,' a Los Angeles County Coroner's Office spokesperson confirmed. 'The cause of death was not blunt force trauma. The file had been sealed by the police, so we cannot disclose the actual cause of death.'

'The manner of death is homicide,' Segreant Rinaldi Thruston of the SMPD confirmed. Little else about the manner of death was revealed at that early juncture of the investigation. They wanted to first learn the identities of the people Juliana associated with.

The secrecy surrounding the case baffled many people and created an even greater public interest in the case. This can cause the imagination to run wild, as we saw with Jane Britton.

SMPD detectives learned that Juliana Redding had lived alone in her apartment on the quiet residential street with her pet dog, a Yorkshire

Terrier named Brutus, which she liked to take for walks at a local dog park. Brutus, thankfully, had been found unharmed inside the apartment with Juliana's body and was placed in an animal shelter.

Police conceded they had no immediate suspects and did not anticipate making any arrests soon. According to Padilla, investigators did not know whether they were looking for one or multiple suspects.

On Tuesday, 18 March 2008, a little more than a full day into the investigation, detectives began interviewing Redding's family, friends, and co-workers, anyone who might know with whom she had been or where she might have gone in the hours before her death. They started with her father, Greg Redding, who almost immediately had a suspect in mind: Juliana's on-and-off boyfriend, John Gilmore.

According to Greg, Juliana and John had been 'on and off' for a year or two.

When interviewed by investigators, John affirmed that he went by Juliana's house the morning after the crime before her body was discovered. He confirmed that he looked through the security door and could see the candle lit on the table. John was known to have a history of violent behaviour. At some point before Juliana's murder, he went into a drunken fit of rage and kicked in the door of her car. Greg also confided in the police that John tried to break into Juliana's apartment. Greg did what every protective father would do and told Juliana to get out of the relationship, warning her that the man was dangerous.

But Juliana did not listen to her father. She stuck with John even if they argued often. They even argued the day before her death.

During the interview, John said that he called Juliana and said, 'I'm gonna (sic) have beers with the boys,' she said, 'Okay, fine', and then hung up on him. This argument only seemed like a minor spat, nothing to write about, but Gilmore admitted that while he had the occasional outburst, he claimed it never became physical. 'Yeah, we would yell. That time I kicked the door, I was pissed. I kicked it a couple times.'[6]

No matter the state of their relationship, John attested that the night Juliana was slain, he and Juliana had each gone their own way. Juliana was with a girlfriend and Gilmore was out with his surfing buddies at a house party several miles away.

The two were still exchanging text messages until around 10.00 pm when Juliana abruptly stopped messaging back.

By the next afternoon, Gilmore became increasingly concerned that he had not heard from Juliana. He called her numerous times, but all attempts were unsuccessful. Juliana's other friends tried to contact her, and in the end, they called her mother. This is where Juliana's mother's concern grew, and she called the police.

Occam's Razor would have looked at John and said the anger made him a potential suspect. Maybe his anger got the better of him. But the police were able to clear John almost immediately. They obtained surveillance footage of him on Saturday night from a convenience store, a Jack in the Box, and a third location. Several people confirmed he was at a house party between 9.44 pm and 10.15 pm. So, that theory is debunked.

A neighbour, Sury Nunez, said that she and Juliana had made plans to play pool the night her body was found, but the outing had not taken place. 'That same night, we were supposed to go out, but we thought she was already out since we saw the lights were off,' Nunez said. 'She was a really lovely girl.'[7]

The dribs and drabs of information being fed to the media from the case were insufficient to satisfy them. It created more questions than answers. Concerned citizens of Santa Monica wanted to know whether a weapon had been used to kill Juliana Redding. Still, the cops would not disclose that information, declaring that they needed to keep that something that only the police and the killer or killers would know.

People who lived in the neighbourhood and were concerned about their safety also wanted to know whether Juliana had been sexually assaulted or if neighbours had heard any screams or other noises indicating foul play. Again, the police would not say. Nor would investigators talk about the evidence they collected from the crime scene or, if any, provide a link to a suspect. They also would not say whether the blood found on the sidewalk outside Juliana's apartment had yielded any clues; instead, they asked the public for any information about the case that might help police solve it.

Juliana's mother spoke favourably about the police work and echoed their sentiments about keeping most of the investigation under wraps.

'We believe the police are doing what they can to solve this case, but we prefer no media attention.' This makes sense. This family has gone through something life-changing, something unimaginable. The last thing they needed was flashing cameras left and right.

Despite the official reticence about the investigation, America's Most Wanted aired an episode about the case. According to AMW, Juliana had indeed died because of blunt force trauma, and the program added that the preliminary investigation revealed that Juliana had not been shot or stabbed. Investigators also told AMW that they were reviewing DNA evidence found at the scene, including the blood evidence found on the sidewalk outside the apartment. AMW also confirmed that there had been no signs of forced entry into Juliana's apartment.

The lab took three months to process all the evidence at the crime scene fully. While the results taking that long is concerning, the results would take the case in a shocking new direction. It was discovered that all the DNA found on Juliana's throat, on her clothes, on the stove, on the doorknob and even on that plate, all belonged to a woman.

We have a beautiful young woman who has been horribly brutalized. She had been strangled, she had been beaten, but the only potential suspect would have been John, who may have had anger issues. But the DNA all came through a woman. Logically, it just did not make any sense.

Authorities began gathering further DNA samples; these individuals included about every female you could imagine in Juliana's life, forty-one females, but each tested negative.

Investigators were left with very few options, so they began to dig deep into Juliana's relationships. The most interesting one? With an older man, a surgeon named Dr Munir Uwaydah.

Dr Uwaydah was described by Alan Jackson as a Lebanese American in his early 40s, an international man of mystery, and a wealthy Los Angeles-based surgeon with valuable real estate all over the world. Uwaydah got his medical degree in Beirut, Lebanon, then completed his training in New York City. At Stanford, he became a surgeon and a thriving medical entrepreneur with several clinics. However, he had a slightly darker side. That darker side involved allegations of fraud.

Dr Uwaydah's multimillion-dollar medical businesses had been under investigation. For instance, there was one case where he conned a company out of a million-dollar CT scanner, never paying for it. The appellate court ordered him to spend almost a million dollars in a judgment.

Regardless of the questions and allegations surrounding his professional life, Dr Uwaydah had an exuberant lifestyle, and he liked his fair share of women, along with his houses, horses, and cars. We already know that Juliana was a stunning girl; many men see beauty as currency, something to take ownership of. Was this Juliana for Dr Uwaydah?

Dr Uwaydah is a powerful man. Whether it's his money, age or position that makes him powerful or a toxic mix of the three, it is undeniable. This is something we need to note for the rest of this chapter. Powerful men are terrifying because they have the expectation that there are no consequences to their actions. Powerful men are narcissistic, and people become commodities to them. A means to an end.

Dr Uwaydah met Juliana in 2007. She was young and beautiful, and he saw her before she glanced at him. Within days, he offered her a job as an assistant. She had no formal medical training, but he paid her a decent salary. He proceeded to sweep her off her feet. While this may seem like the start of a romance, their relationship exemplifies the delicate boundary between romance and obsession.

In an essay titled "Sex, Power and the Systems that Enable Men like Harvey Weinstein," psychologist Dacher Keltner explains that powerful men also sexualize their work, looking for opportunities for sexual trysts and affairs, and along the way leer inappropriately, stand too close, and touch for too long daily, thus crossing the lines of decorum – and worse.[8]

Kelly Duncan, once a contestant on The Bachelor, was a close friend of Juliana's. She was also interviewed by police. 'She ended up living in his house for a while… as it turned into something…' They began dating, and Juliana even told her parents about him. He was no longer Munir, the boss. He was Munir, the man I am dating. She even moved into his lavish Beverly Hills home.

According to Kelly Duncan, everything looked like sunshine and roses, but the relationship became uncomfortable. 'The guy's obsessed with her … she was giving him the time of day, and he loved it. … he loved having her around, she was like arm candy, he was obsessed. I could see it in his eyes trying to, like, buy her.'

Money aside, when you have a huge age gap in a relationship like this one, power always goes to the older person. The younger person may feel that they are indebted to the older person, there is an imbalance of power, and the younger partner is seen as being taken advantage of. There will always be people who project a dynamic that serves them.

Munir has attempted to romance and enchant Juliana with his wealth and gifts, making her almost indebted to him. Greg even confirmed during his police interview that Munir would buy Juliana a Lamborghini for her 21st birthday. Which would be terrifying for anyone.

The car must have been the straw that broke the camel's back.

She turned down the Lamborghini, and, wanting to cool things down a bit, in September, she moved out of the Beverly Hills home and into the bungalow, paid for by her father, in Santa Monica.

Juliana did not immediately cut ties with Dr Uwaydah; she was planning a birthday trip to Las Vegas with her girlfriends and the doctor. So, the doctor tried a different approach to encroach Juliana back into his palm, her father.

During his police interview, Greg said to investigators 'he told me, "Greg, I can offer your daughter the world." He even offered Greg a pretty good job, over $400,000 a year working as a pharmacist in one of Dr Uwayadah's businesses.

Greg Redding didn't buy it, and he already suspected that the doctor had some murky business dealings, but he wanted to find out more about a man who seemed to be offering the world to him and his daughter. So, he did his own private investigation, which came to a head in Las Vegas.

The party took a chartered plane to Las Vegas with several of Juliana's girlfriends. The celebration didn't even lift the ground when Juliana's dad called her to confirm something horrifying.

'Munir is married in another country.'

Uwaydah was married to a woman in Lebanon, and they had three children, which was news to Juliana. Rightfully, she was furious and confronted him in Vegas. Juliana finally broke up with him, and five months later, she was dead. If the evidence allowed it to, Occam's Razor would give an explanation that allows the fewest assumptions: Uwaydah murdered her. But we have a dilemma: the DNA evidence and the fact that it points to a woman.

Juliana and her girlfriends got a separate hotel room, and the following day, they flew back home; that ended up being the end of their relationship. That was October 2007, but whilst Juliana may have been done with Dr Uwaydah, that didn't mean he was done with her.

Kelly Duncan says Juliana told her that what started with persistent text messages from Uwaydah, which moved to him stalking her, he would drive by her house and show up at places she frequented around town. Uwaydah also continued to pursue Juliana's father, Greg Redding.

'... he actually flew me out for [a] Christmas present to Vegas to watch the Mayweather fight. Those tickets were like $1,500 bucks a piece.' Surprisingly, despite his reservations about his daughter's relationship with the doctor, Greg continued to navigate his professional relationship with Uwaydah. Perhaps it was the lure of that six-figure salary or all the trappings that went with it. Uwaydah promised him the world. A car, a chance to stay at his Beverly Hills house, you name it.

But in March 2008, the deal fell apart, and less than a week later, Juliana's body was found in her bedroom. Could the broken business deal between Dr Uwaydah and Juliana's father be the motive for this murder? Or could it be Uwaydah's bruised ego after Juliana's rejection? Investigators threw out the 'bruised ego' theory and went with the broken deal.

Nevertheless, the investigators were now enraptured on Uwaydah, but the DNA at the crime scene was female, and Uwaydah was proven to be out of the country at the time of the murder. No matter how rich you are, flying back from one country and back again to murder someone isn't plausible. But paying someone to murder you? A possibility.

The investigators were still testing the DNA of women who may have had a foot in Juliana's life. Only when they looked at female associates of Uwaydah's, they happened upon Kelly Soo Park.

Kelly Soo Park, forty-seven, was a licensed real estate broker born and educated in Southern California. She was an employee of Dr Uwaydah's and was said to work closely with him on many of his business deals. Police followed Park one day and picked up one of her cigarette butts.

Mouths dropped at the results.

The DNA from Park's cigarette matched the DNA at the crime scene.

Do we know if Juliana had ever met or even known of Park before that night? No. The only connection between them was Dr Munir Uwaydah. He dated one of them and employed her, and he employed the other.

But why? Why would Park attack a woman she didn't even know? The only thing to do was put a microscope on Kelly Soo Park, and they found that she was deeply entrenched. Munir may have hired her as an enforcer, intimidator, or muscle. Munir would frequently brag that she was his 'female James Bond.' She is nearly six feet tall and known to be quite intimidating.

Cindy Ogden, a real estate agent who had several deals and business disputes with Dr Uwaydah, said that when she saw Park for the first time, she presented herself like a thug. Ogden was brokering a multimillion-dollar commercial real estate deal with Dr Uwaydah when she said Uwaydah used Kelly Soo Park and several other women as intimidators, almost like a 'Charlie's Angels' scenario. She says she felt they were pressuring her to come to their terms. She never did.

This is what the investigators say happened to Juliana on March 6th. According to the prosecution, Kelly Soo Park went to Juliana's house as ordered by D. Uwaydah to scare her and her father back into the business deal. What they would argue at the trial is that Kelly Soo Park was muscle for Dr Uwaydah. With the backstory of Kelly Soo Park and the undeniable DNA evidence, on March 17th 2010, Park was arrested for the murder of Juliana Redding.

She pleaded not guilty and was given a $3.5 million bail.

Someone paid her bail, but prosecutors could not prove that that someone was Dr Uwaydah. However, there was no doubt that other financial transfers had been made prior. So, the means were there.

At the beginning of June 2008, for the next 18 months, Kelly Soo Park was given over a *million dollars* by Munir Uwaydah. This is inconsistent with her ongoing normal employment, and unless you are on 'Selling Sunshine', you do not make that sort of money being a real estate broker. If you do, then I am in the wrong job.

That would be too much of a salary for any standard job unless, as the prosecution would argue, it was a payoff for the murder of Juliana.

But Kelly Soo Park would face her trial alone. Two days after she was arrested, Dr Munir Uwaydah conveniently vanished. He was believed to be over 7000 miles away in Beirut.

Three years would pass before Kelly Soo Park was tried in court. Alan Jackson, the original prosecutor, had moved on to private practice. Replacing him was Stacy Weise.

In May 2013, the trial engrossed national and local media, drawn to a case originating as a whodunit. Journalists, supporters and relatives of both victim and defendant arrived each day at Los Angeles' main criminal courthouse in the heart of downtown. The imposing nineteen-story concrete building has been home to some of the country's most high-profile criminal cases, including the 1995 O.J. Simpson murder trial and the 2011 case of Dr Conrad Murray, charged and convicted of involuntary manslaughter in the death of pop icon Michael Jackson. The amount of weight this place holds is indescribable, and now it was home to a frankly confounding case.

Before the trial commenced, the court made two critical decisions. One damaged the prosecution and the other the defence. The prosecution had to dispute all the allegations about Park operating as an enforcer on behalf of Uwaydah. The judge said they could not bring the allegation in as they had not proved she had ever acted violently. The jury never heard the theory. This was detrimental for them and this case because what are they supposed to argue now?

It was a significant setback, but the defence was also dealt a blow when the judge disallowed one of their strongest arguments. They had wanted to argue that Juliana's off-and-on-again boyfriend, John Gilmore, was the killer. But, according to the prosecutors, Gilmore had a rock-solid alibi and was immediately cleared of any wrongdoing because there were videos of him that night at several locations. The investigators were very comfortable. They knew precisely where John Gilmore was; he was not at Juliana's apartment. The boyfriend did it. It would have been the ideal theory with the most superficial assumptions, but the evidence was stacked against it.

When the trial finally began, the prosecution opened with what they believed was an unimpeachable DNA case. Stacy Wiese addressed the court; 'the killer, the defendant, got her DNA on Juliana's tank top during the struggle and during the murder.' Her DNA was on the front door, the locks, and Juliana's telephone when she stopped her from calling the police. It was on the front and the back of Juliana's T-shirt. Kelly Soo Park's DNA was on Juliana's throat. The case should have been a slam dunk. Emphasis on should.

There was even a single but telling drop of blood found in a fingerprint on a plate in the sink. It was from Kelly Soo Park's left thumb.

The defence did not even try to argue against the DNA. There was no point. Instead, they attempted to dispute how it got there in the first place.

Defence attorney George Beuhler waited until closing arguments to launch his attack.

'...when I touch an object, if I leave my DNA, then someone else can come along and touch that object and pick up my DNA. They may go to touch another object; leave my DNA, and I never touched that object.' It was a very bold argument. They argued that the DNA had been transferred from somewhere else to the murder scene.[9]

In his closing argument, Beuhler proposed an entirely new theory of crime, complete with a mysterious killer. He said that they had a killer who had a rag, and with that rag, he was wiping places to get rid of his fingerprints. Unbeknownst to him, he has Park's DNA on that rag.

The real killer could have cleaned up the crime scene, expunged it of all DNA, then inadvertently planted Kelly Soo Park's DNA by using a towel that Kelly may have used once five months earlier at Dr Uwaydah's Beverly Hills house -- a place Park had visited, and Juliana had once lived.

In my opinion, this theory is inconceivable. It is exceedingly unlikely that Juliana brought a tower from Dr Uwaydah's house that belonged to Park and it managed to leave that much DNA. DNA under her fingernails from a towel? Blood. From a towel? If we went further and said maybe someone wanted to implicate Park in this murder by murdering Juliana and spreading her DNA all over the crime scene, we must ask the question as to how they got the DNA in the first place, why they would want to do this, and who the murderer really is.

But Beuhler did not have to prove his theory. He just had to raise reasonable doubt. He told the jurors not to be fooled by the DNA, and that Park did not even know Juliana. She and Dr Uwaydah had no known history of violence.

He also argued that Park was not strong enough; she may have had 3 inches and 40 pounds on Juliana, but it was not enough to account for this carnage.

And with the million dollars Kelly Soo Park received from Dr Uwaydah showed that she was a successful businesswoman. Nothing more.

For more than a week, Juliana's family and friends came to court, reliving every horrible detail of her death. Now, they would wait another seven long days for the jury to render its verdict.

Finally, the jury spoke.

Not guilty.

Park gasped and cried in the downtown Los Angeles courtroom as the verdict on the second-degree murder charge was read within an hour after the reading of the first-degree murder verdict.

But Juliana's friends and family got the last word. When court was dismissed, a group seated in the gallery started yelling at Park, screaming 'Murderer!' and 'She knows she did it!'

It's like I said at the beginning of this chapter, in a case like this, where there is so much evidence, it almost seemed like the defence was working to exonerate a guilty person, but they may say, why should they believe Park is guilty, the prosecution did not meet their burden of proof. Their version of the truth won.

Two years and two months after her murder acquittal, Kelly Soo Park was arrested, and she found herself back in court.[10]

This time, as Dr Uwaydah's office manager. Park and a dozen other associates pleaded not guilty to conspiracy, lying to patients, disfiguring some in botched surgeries, and cheating insurance companies out of $150 million. Dr Uwaydah was not present; his whereabouts are unknown.

Uwaydah and his staff allegedly tricked twenty-one people into thinking he would perform their operations. Instead, they were done by a physician's assistant -- which is against the law and a terrifying misuse of power.

Attorney George Buehler, who stood by Park's side at her murder trial, was with her again when she was arraigned for fraud.

He believed she wasn't guilty then, and she wasn't guilty now. She was just of interest because of her acquittal. Park's bail was initially set at $10 million. It was later reduced when the court dismissed the charges relating to disfiguring patients. In April 2016, Kelly Soo Park was released on bail of more than $1.5 million. No date has been set for the fraud trial. Dr Munir Uwaydah's California medical license has been cancelled.

In a sense, Juliana's case could be treated as unsolved, but in my opinion, this case was a horrific injustice. This case defies all Occam's Razor logic. John Gilmore, the boyfriend, was alleged to be prone to instances of anger and rage, but he wasn't there on the night of the murder. Even if he had a chance to slip away undetected, his DNA was nowhere near the crime scene. Kelly Soo Park's was. Even if Juliana's involvement with Munir Uwaydah and the incorporation of his 'muscle' to kill her seems like something out of a Gillian Flynn novel, it was the best-case scenario because of the abundance of DNA evidence.

Occam's Razor refers to the theory that makes the fewest assumptions. Additionally, it does not refer to one theory in a case- it is a guideline used to compare competing hypotheses. The idea is you take two theories; here, we take Kelly Soo Park being the assailant and the other being DNA transfer from a seemingly random killer, and you ask, 'Which of these makes the fewest assumptions?' The one you're left with is the more plausible of the two. That's why it's called the 'law of parsimony'- it's a suggestive rule, not a fact.

But the court case was the biggest middle finger in Occam's Razor's face. How the jury was convinced that the DNA could be transferred by a random assailant did not make any sense. Because then further assumptions would have to be made about how the killer came across Kelly Soo Park's DNA in the first place. And then, who could the assailant have been in the first place?

Really, if Occam's Razor had been applied, then the evidence would be stacked against Park, and the explanation with the fewest assumptions would be that she killed Juliana Redding and should have been brought to justice.

It is undeniable that the slaying of Juliana Redding and the outcome, or lack thereof, is disquieting, and in a sense, maybe Occam's Razor could have been used to provide some sort of outcome for her family. Sadly, Juliana joins a line of women whose perpetrators have not been brought to justice and are still walking free.

Chapter Five

The Kidnap and Murder of Jacob Wetterling

T rue crime narratives are never linear. There are always loose threads reaching out to others whose stories inevitably end up intertwined and tangled, with no way to come undone.

Jacob Wetterling's story is about Jacob Wetterling, but it is also about his family and all of the other boys who were assaulted, and it is also about Jared Scheierl.

In 1986, St. Joseph, Minnesota, was your typical small, rural town with a population of two thousand people. It was safe. Which is the bare minimum parents want for their children: a safe place for them to grow up. Kids would ride their bikes out of town, down remote roads, and walk to the store. They would simply exist. Parents did not think their children were in any danger.

But if you were a young boy between eleven and twelve, you were in possible danger. Between 1986 and 1988, the town of Paynesville was victim to a cluster of assaults on young boys. There were a total of eight assaults on seven different boys; one of them was assaulted twice.

These attacks had very similar MOs; the boys had the same characteristics, and the assailant was described as a white man in his thirties, approx. 5ft 9in in height. With a slightly heavier build and wearing a mask. All of the assaults happened in public places, when the boys were walking home, riding their bikes or hanging out with their friends.

The perpetrator would knock them off their bikes or drag them away and attempt to grope them over or under their clothing. He would sometimes ask the boys their ages and/or threaten to kill them. During one attack on 30 November 1986, he told the boy to keep lying down, or he would 'blow your head off.'

During another attack that took place on 14 February 1987, a boy and his friend were in a stairwell of an apartment complex when one of the boys was attacked. The man threw the boy down the stairs, and the boy started screaming, but the man told him to keep quiet, or he would kill him.[1] He then asked the boy what grade he was in and proceeded to grope him over and under his clothing. After that, he took the boy's wallet and left.

Just three months later, the same boy was attacked again. On 17 May 1987, the boy was riding his bike in town when the perpetrator knocked him off the bike. He then proceeded to grope him, to which the boy screamed, 'What are you doing? You already got me!'

The man fled on foot, and in the rush, he dropped his baseball cap. The cap was handed over to the police and the Bureau of Criminal Apprehension for testing, where they identified three samples of DNA from the cap. Three or more individuals, more than likely one of them was from one of the boys who was attacked, but who were the others?

Regrettably, this was not an end to the attacks. 12-year-old Jared Scheierl was kidnapped and sexually assaulted near Cold Spring on 13 January 1989, six days before his 13th birthday. It is important to note that Cold Water was twelve to fifteen minutes away from other attacks in Paynesville.[2]

It was nightfall at 9.00 pm when Jared and his friend Corey Eskelson walked home from the local skating rink. The two boys lived in opposite directions and split up when needed. When Jared was walking home, a man pulled up in a blue car and asked for directions. Then the man forced him into his car. He said he had a gun and wasn't afraid to use it.

He forced Jared into the backseat and started to drive. Despite his terror, Jared observed the drive and noted his surroundings. He noticed a handheld walkie-talkie radio on the passenger seat. The man caught him eyeing it and threatened him with the gun again. 'Don't try anything stupid.'

After about fifteen minutes of driving, the man stopped on a gravel road. He got into the backseat and told Jared to remove his snowmobile suit and pull his pants and underwear down. Jared, terrified, did what he was told.

The man then sexually assaults Jared. After he was done, he returned Jared his snowmobile suit but kept his underwear as a souvenir. He dropped Jared off two miles from his house, but before he let him go, he says, 'You're lucky to be alive, and if the police find out about this, I will find you after school and kill you.'

'I think I slept on my parent's bedroom floor for the first year,' Jared explains, '(That is) the level of fear you go through.'

Remember Corey, Jared's friend? Well, Jared did not go to school the day after his attack. Corey did not know why, and that day, FBI agents came into his classroom asking Corey for his hat. They did not say why they wanted it, but he gave it anyway. He later found out that Jared had told investigations that the man who kidnapped him had worn a hat that looked like Corey's.

You would hope the investigators would have talked to Corey about that night on the off chance he saw something, but Corey revealed that the FBI did not ask him a single question. He had never been interviewed by law enforcement.

Jared described his assailant to authorities as short, maybe five-six or so. Around 170 pounds matches the height and build of the man responsible for the other attacks. Coincidence? I think not. Jared also said that the man wore military-style camouflage clothing, had a deep, raspy voice, and drove a blue car.

Jared's observation skills paid off. It was dark out, so he couldn't see much, but he remembers they went over railroad tracks and weren't on pavement anymore when they turned onto a gravel road. Investigators took Jared for a ride to see if he'd remember where the man took him. They had him lie in the back seat of one of their cars and cover his eyes. Jared ended up directing them to a spot between Cold Spring, where Jared lives, and the town of Paynesville, where those other attacks occurred.

Just three days after Jared's attack, a deputy with the Sterns County Sheriff's office put forward a possible suspect. Danny Heinrich, who happened to be from Paynesville. He was about 5ft 5, was a stocky build, and he happened to drive a blue car. Jared and his family had not been made aware that his attack was a similar MO to the Paynesville attack. No links had been made, and Jared did not know that other boys had been through the same thing he did.

One thing law enforcement did when they had Danny Heinrich as a possible suspect was put together a lineup. The lineup consisted of Danny

Heinrich and other men for Jared to see if he could identify one of them as his attacker. Jared picked out two of the men he thought resembled the man who attacked him. One of those men was Danny Heinrich. Now, I, along with others, would think that maybe they would show this lineup to the boys of Paynesville, the ones who were attacked there, but they don't.

The day after Jared picked out two men from the lineup, detectives found Heinrich's car parked outside his work. Jared told investigators the vehicle had a luggage rack and a blue interior. But Heinrich's car did not have a luggage rack. And the inside of the vehicle was more grey than blue. However, it was darker when the attack happened. And it is pretty close to blue in the dark! Jared maybe thought he saw a luggage rack, or maybe Heinrich even removed it, but Heinrich was never charged, and neither was anyone else. Then, an attack happens again nine months later.

Jacob Irwin Wetterling was born on 17 February 1978. He was 11 years old and lived with his older sister Amy, younger brother and sister Trevor and Carmen, mother and father Patty and Jerry Wetterling.

The family of six lived in St Joseph, Minnesota. Jacob's parents, Patty and Jerry Wetterling were said to be living the American dream. They had a beautiful home and lived an everyday family life. Jacob, who had sandy brown hair, blue eyes and a big smile, adored sports, particularly football and hockey, and he enjoyed fishing with his dad. He was an enthusiastic little boy. He loved dogs and was musically gifted. Having mastered the piano, he was then learning how to play the trombone. Jacob's mum, Patty, said that one thing that was important to him was fairness. One day, she asked Jacob, who played in goals in football games, if it had upset him when someone scored, and he replied, 'No if it went in, it was a good shot. If I saved it, it was a good save.' He applied this notion to everything he did in sports and life.

St Joseph's Township was situated in a fairly rural area and, at the time, was considered safe by many people. The population on Saturday was 2500 people. And as small communities go, everybody knew everybody, or so they thought. Without the Wetterling family realising it, their semblance of safety was about to be shattered, sparking a twenty-seven-year-long mystery that would ultimately change their lives.

On a warm October night in 1989, just before moonrise, three boys, including Jacob, rode home on their bikes and scooters along a dead-end rural road from the Tom Thumb store in St. Joseph, where they had rented *The Naked Gun*.

Patty initially wanted her children to stay home that evening. She and Jerry were at a dinner party when Jacob called her at 9.00 pm to ask if he and his brother, Trevor, could ride to the video store. Since it was already dark, the boys would have to leave their little sister alone, and their older sister was at a sleepover, so she said no. But the resourceful kids called their father to hopefully get a different answer. They assured him that they would wear reflective vests and use flashlights on the mile-long bike ride to the store, and as for Carmen, they would get their 14-year-old neighbour to babysit. Jerry agreed. After all, this was supposed to be a safe place to live. So the Wetterling brothers and their friend Aaron set off.

After renting *The Naked Gun* on VHS, the trio mounted their bicycles and pedalled back, but they had not gotten far when a masked man emerged from a driveway and ordered the boys to abandon their bikes in a ditch and to lie face down on the asphalt. He then asked them their ages.

Trevor was told to run into the woods and not look back, or he would be shot. The man then told Jacob and Aaron to turn around so he could inspect their faces before ordering 11-year-old Aaron to leave as well. Trevor and Aaron were given a lifeline and rushed home to notify the neighbours. Aaron did look back for a glimpse and saw the man grab Jacob's arm and pick him up. That was the last time anyone saw Jacob alive.

Aaron and Trevor ran the remaining two blocks to the Wetterling home and told the babysitter hurriedly what happened. She called her father, Merlyn, who called the police. Merlyn was also the one who notified Jacob's parents and told them they needed to come home. They left the dinner party immediately without even saying goodbye. Patty said it felt like the longest car ride in existence. When Merlyn made the 911 call between 9.00 pm and 9.30 pm that night, Jacob had been missing for fifteen minutes.

Fifteen minutes does not seem that long, but fifteen minutes is an excruciating and pivotal amount of time when a child is missing. Robert

Lowery Jr., vice president of the Missing Children Division of the National Centre for Missing and Exploited Children, says 'when it comes to missing children, time is the enemy, seconds count, hours count, if that child is going to be killed, it is going to happen within the first few hours.'[3]

The dispatcher spoke about Merlyn and Trevor to try and get a description of a masked man whilst officers were en route to the property. Trevor said the man was the same height as Merlyn, roughly 5ft 10", wore a black mask and spoke like he had a cold. The dispatcher suggested that Jacob may have run off into the woods shortly after the boys had gotten lost. But Trevor was adamant that he had been taken.

At this point, the first officer, Deputy Bruce Bechtold, arrived at the Wetterling home. He asked the boys to go with him to the abduction site, but they were too scared to leave without Merlyn. At the same time, Patty and Jerry rushed home, and when they arrived, the deputy, the boys and Merlyn were still there. Trevor and Aaron were very obviously still shaken. Trevor talked nonstop, telling them everything that happened and everything he could remember. But Aaron just stood in the corner, biting his nails. Patty described Aaron as if it was like he wanted to disappear.

We know that kids will be kids; sometimes, they may take pranks too far or end up doing something wrong and trying to hide it. So investigators wanted to ensure this wasn't some elaborate joke or prank. They sat the boys down and asked them questions. 'Are you sure you weren't just playing with a gun and Jacob got hurt, and you're afraid to tell? Or are you sure Jacob just didn't run away?' But they were unyielding that he was taken.

Officers responded to the abduction site within six minutes. Troublingly, they did not find a single sign of life, despite the optimism of Stearns County Sheriff Charlie Graft, who believed that 'within a few hours we (they) would get it taken care of'.

Jacob's parents were advised by the police to stay home and not partake in the search just in case Jacob came home.

Graft saw the boys' bikes in the ditch and immediately called for backup, including help from the F.B.I. Throughout the night, the officers searched for Jacob with flashlights, and a state patrol helicopter searched the dense woods with a flood light, but no luck. But searchers on the ground did come across something in the gravel driveway, across the street from the abduction site, some tyre tracks and some shoe prints. Initially, they did not know what to make of them as the boys did not mention seeing a car, and it is not unusual for a driveway to have tyre tracks. Investigators did not know if the tracks had anything to do with the investigation initially. But, looking at the abduction site, a rural area with no other buildings and in a small town, you would be seen if you were running with a child on foot. Having a car for a quick getaway seems plausible and should be considered.

Presumably, some of the tracks and prints were made by the perpetrator. Figuring out which, with no idea of the kind of shoe he was wearing or the type of tyre on his car, if he even had a car, was the objective. The police needed the gravel to tell them a story, but it was as comprehensive as reading in a language you have never been taught.

The issue with tyre tracks and shoe prints is that they fall into the forensic categories of 'pattern evidence' and are difficult to identify. They are also difficult to document through casting and even more challenging to match to a potential suspect. They cannot simply be loaded onto a computer and then presented with analysed data of the car's make, model, and year the tracks identify. That is the reality now, let alone in 1989 when the World Wide Web was created.

The search was called off at 3.00 am. At this point, there may not have been a chance to find Jacob alive.

The long gravel driveway across the spot from where Jacob was abducted curves around and leads to a white farmhouse with a clothesline out front. Inside the farmhouse was 34-year-old Dan Rassier. He was home alone. At the time, Rassier lived with his parents, which was perceived as odd, and was a music teacher who taught many children in the local area. He was a key witness from the very beginning. That night, he was engrossed in typing index cards to catalogue his enormous music collection. Still, his attention was drawn to the window at some point by the spectacle of a tan Monte Carlo-type car barrelling up the driveway.

The house cannot be seen from the main road, known as 91st and 16th Avenues, so sometimes people drive up unaware they're headed for a dead end. But this car was unusual.

Later, after nightfall, Rassier was alerted again by the barking of his dog, Smokey. He looked out the window to see another car, this one smaller and darker, with headlights close together, driving fast up the driveway and turning around the same way the first one had. He acknowledged the strange coincidence of it but went to bed anyway.

The next thing Rassier remembers is Smokey barking again. He looked out to see flashlights moving near the family's mammoth woodpile. Thinking the trespassers might be thieves, he dialled 911 at about 10.45. That's when he found out from a dispatcher that a child had been abducted. Rassier said he went outside and spoke briefly to a Stearns County sheriff's deputy, saw about ten officers engaged in the search and poked around some outbuildings before heading back inside.

They end up not finding any clues or anything on Dan's property. But they don't just leave it at that. The morning after Jacob's abduction, police showed up at the school to talk with him. According to APM reports, they looked at the tyres of his car and looked in his trunk but found nothing. They leave after finding nothing, but they keep Dan on their radar.[4]

The search resumed the next morning at 8.00 am, and at this point, the entire town of St. Joseph knew about it.

Jacob went missing on Sunday, 22 October. On 24 October, at 3.40 pm, a local high school sophomore and his father went to the Stearn's County Sheriff's Office asking to meet with an investigator. When they meet, the boy confides in the investigator about at least eight assaults in the nearby town of Paynesville, which is only fifteen minutes away from St. Joseph. Concerningly, the investigators were not aware of these attacks.

The boy was a witness to two of the assaults, depicting that a man grabbed two boys off their bikes and threatened them with a knife. A very similar MO. The boy and his father pleaded with them and urged them to talk with the Paynesville Police Department, who were aware of those attacks in their town. The Occam's Razor way of thinking may be that the officers would connect these attacks, at least look into it. Especially since they were geographically close together. However, the investigators do not pursue this potential lead for reasons I am unaware of.

On 25 October 1989, three days after Jacob disappeared, a prayer vigil was held at the St Joseph church, where over 500 people attended. Graft reveals that he is sure it was a sex offender who took Jacob, and he believes they have likely left the area, suggesting that Jacob could even be dead.

In the meantime, Patty and Jerry try to garner as much publicity for Jacob as possible. On 26 October, four days after Jacob was taken, an episode of A Current Affair was released with Mari Povich as host.

Patty pleaded for Jacob's safe return; 'this shouldn't happen anywhere [...] who would take a child away from its parents?'[5]

She said, 'We taught him that people are good. We've worked for peace all our lives, and this is a really violent act, and I don't understand it. [...] He's a survivor.'[6]

During the same episode, Aaron and Trevor walked the abduction site, revealing the intricate details of the abduction, including what the assailant looked like and what he said. At this point, there was a lot of media coverage, which meant that authorities received a plethora of tips. 300 in total, but none of them led to Jacob. But there was still hope he would come back alive.

After the same four days, Minneapolis and St. Paul business leaders offered a $100,000 reward for Jacob's safe return. Deputies searched on horseback for clues, and the FBI had 20 agents assigned to the case. On 27 October 1989, the Governor of Minnesota activated the National Guard, the State Patrol and the Department of Natural Resources to search a 700 square-mile radius in the hopes of finding this boy.

The Wetterlings even do another interview on CBS *This Morning*, hoping to get the word out to everyone possible. Radio stations across the entire state played his favourite song, 'Listen' by Red Grammer. With the song, they played a message for Jacob from his mother in the hopes that he would hear it and it would lead him home.

About a week after his abduction, thousands of people came together to form a human chain that stretched for three miles. They walked down the main road in the cold, including Minnesota Twins baseball players wearing blue warm-up jackets with Jacob's initials.

This is just a fraction of the publicity this case was getting, and the Wetterlings were hoping that all of it would get the lead they need, the lead to Jacob. The community of St. Joesph were also looking for him without the assistance of law enforcement. They searched roads, ditches, abandoned buildings, barns, fields, the woods, anywhere and everywhere.

Flyers were made with Jacob's photo and description on them. They put them everywhere: in stores, power poles, and parked cars. And then came Jacob's Hope. People would wear white ribbons pinned to their shirts to symbolise hope for Jacob and his safe return.

We must remember that the police keep Dan Rassier as a person of interest. They put much effort into him and showed up at Dan's farm a week after Jacob's disappearance. This time, they do a more thorough search of the property, particularly in his bedroom. After that night, the police gave him a lie-detector test, which he passed. They have nothing to arrest him for, so they let him go. At this point, they might want to consider looking at other theories.

In the week that followed, a sketch was released to the public. Investigators received a tip of a suspicious man scene at the convenience store where the boys rented the movie from on the night of Jacob's abduction. They've been trying to find this man but can't track him down. They describe him as a white man in his 50s, about 200 pounds, with white hair, and as glaring at customers.

Then, about a week later, police released two more sketches. One is of a man who was heard talking about the abduction two weeks after it happened in the same convenience store the boys were in. The second sketch is of a man thought to have tried to abduct a boy in New Brighton, Minnesota, which is about an hour from St. Joseph, where Jacob was taken.

These two sketches match the previous sketch of the man in the convenience store glaring at people. This is when even more tips came flying in and phone calls. Sheriff Graft ended up having to set up a 24-hour call centre just to be able to keep up with all the leads that were pouring in. The awkward thing about this was that every single minute detail was publicised. Investigators would get a tip about something like a white van, and the people would start seeing white vans everywhere! One tip about a white van would turn into hundreds of tips about white vans.

Some people would even call the Wetterlings directly with leads. So the sheriff gave them a separate phone to record those calls, which is stressful at home because they get no sense of peace. They get people who pretend to be the kidnapper on the phone and people who pretend to be Jacob, but they cannot answer the phone in case they forsake something vital.

Back to Dan Rassier, three to four weeks after Jacob was taken, they hypnotised him. Often a tool used to jog someone's memory, detectives drove Dan from his home in St. Joseph to the Twin Cities to get him to recall details from that night to better describe the car and the licence plate. They kept pressing him, But all he could come up with was that it was dark in colour, maybe blue. He couldn't give them any more details.

What he did remember, though, was seeing a person in the car's passenger seat, a woman or maybe a child. But afterwards, Dan says he isn't sure if that was even a real memory or if he just sort of made it up while he was under that hypnosis. The police couldn't arrest Dan, so they had to let him go. And again, he was still on their radar as time passed. And unfortunately, they don't get any closer to finding Jacob as time passes.

Almost a whole month after Jacob went missing, six Minnesota Bureau of Criminal Apprehension agents and five FBI agents were taken off the case. I am unsure why. However, they are not stopping the search for Jacob. Ten days after removing those agents, investigators released a new sketch of the man they sought. This sketch is more accurate and detailed; they hope someone will recognise it.

Jacob's parents are doing everything they can to look for him. Jerry even contacts psychics to see if they can help, sending them items of Jacob to see if they can determine his whereabouts. Approximately a month after Jacob was abducted, investigators spent two days searching an area near Mason City, Iowa, which was prompted by a lead from a psychic Jerry had contacted, but nothing was found.

This is a bit concerning because, at this stage of the investigation, investigators have not talked to the Wetterling neighbours, but they were chasing leads from psychics?

Significantly, in mid-December, FBI agents met with Jared Scheierl. Do you remember Jared? The 12-year-old boy was assaulted near Cold Spring in January of that year. When Jared heard about Jacob's abduction, his heart sank.

Immediately, he thought of the man who attacked him. He says, 'There were details that I recognised right away. Some of the phrases were similar, and the description of the voice was similar.'

Jared was helpful with the investigators, which is impressive, considering he was a child and most likely traumatised. He detailed the man who kidnapped and assaulted him, and a sketch was created. One would think that investigators would be kind to a twelve-year-old boy who was kidnapped and assaulted and was assisting them on the case, but according to NPR News, Jared recalls how they were pretty rude and, to him, pushy. He was interviewed multiple times after Jacob's abduction, and he placed a poignant interview in December 1989, where they accused Jared of knowing the man who did this to him. They would pressure him, saying, 'We know who did this to you, now tell us who it is […] if you do not tell us who this man is, we will never find Jacob.' Jared says those words stuck with him forever.[7]

Jared broke down in tears during the interview with investigators because he didn't know who did this to him. It was as if they forgot he was a child. His parents were not allowed to be in the room with him either, and when he walked out with his tears, his parents were livid. They told investigators that enough is enough and no more interviews will be done. His parents meant it so much that they moved from Cold Spring to Paynesville.

A few days after Jared's interview, the FBI returned to Danny Heinrich, eleven months after he was last interviewed. They interview him again, but again, he denies having any knowledge of Jacob's abduction or of what happened to Jared. He only lives about 30 miles from St. Joseph, where Jacob was taken. But they can't prove anything. He denies knowing anything about the kidnappings. So again, they just have to let him go. But he is still on their radar.

Do you know how the investigators were tipped off about the Paynesville attacks by the high school student and his father two days after Jacob's disappearance? The police did not follow this lead until two and a half months later.

On 5 January 1990, they spoke with Paynesville police. And guess who they are led back to again? Danny Heinrich. He was a suspect in the Paynesville assaults. The Paynesville police department says Stearns County officers should retake a good look at him. Occam's Razor must be screaming right now.

A few days later, they question Danny again and take photographs of the tyres on his blue Ford EXP. The tyres on his car are Sears Brand, and the crime scene tracks are from a Sears brand tyre. Danny was very cooperative and even consented to them searching his vehicle. The investigator concludes that Heinrich's tyres are consistent with the tyre tracks and the scene. They even look at the soles of Heinrich's shoes for analysis to see if they can get an accurate or exact match, and guess what? They also come back as a match. Danny also strongly resembled the sketch Jared Scheierl helped investigators put together.

What investigators started doing was putting Danny under surveillance. They began the surveillance on 12 January 1990, at 08.18 pm. Immediately, they see him get into his car, so they tail him. Danny does not make himself appear not guilty, so to speak. He is aware that he is being followed because he makes numerous random turns on roads outside of Paynesville, and within twenty minutes, he turns off his lights, and investigators end up losing him.

Over the next two days, investigators continue to tail him. They follow him home to local bars, and then, for some unforeseen reason, they stop. They only followed him for three days. The question is, would an innocent man take manoeuvres to get away from the police?

Nevertheless, they do gain access to Danny's 1987 Mercury Topaz, the car he owned around Jared's attack. At this point, Danny no longer owns the vehicle, so they have to search for it. They had Jared sit at the back and asked him how similar the car was to the one from their attack. Jared says it is like an eight or a nine on a scale of one to ten, which is very similar.

Around a week or so later, on 24 January 1990, investigators searched Heinrich's home, which was owned by his father. He had lived there since November 1989, a month after Jacob disappeared. What they are looking for is Jacob, his clothing, a gun, any incriminating documents, or anything to give an inclination towards Jacob's disappearance.

They find two police scanners, lists of scanner frequencies, a pair of boots, and some of Danny's clothing, all of which they confiscated during the search. Danny does attempt to tell investigators that when the child was taken, he was at home, nowhere near St Joseph, which may have worked, until the investigators find something undoubtedly incriminating.

A truck in Danny's home containing photos of children. One is of a boy with a towel wrapped around himself, and another is a picture of a boy in his underwear.

Danny objects to the investigators taking these photos, and later, when he is asked about them again, he says, 'I do not have the pictures anymore because I burned them.' I want to know why the investigators did not think it was a good idea to have these confiscated in the first place, primarily if Danny could not provide a reason for having those photos in the first place.[8]

On 26 January, two days after searching Danny's home, investigators have him stand in a line up for three boys to pick out. Two of the boys had reported seeing a suspicious man in a car near the Wetterling's home, and the third boy was Jared. Regrettably, none of the boys picked out any of the men as the one they saw or, in Jared's perspective, who attacked him. But trauma is a powerful thing, and the police have taken their time in this investigation. This was a year after Jared's assault, so memories and faces are going to be blurred.

Moreover, appearances can be changed within a year. In 2018, a man named Don Gudmunson, Stern County Sheriff, who we will return to later, said that investigators should have gotten Danny to speak in front of the boys, to say lines that the attack had said to see if the boys recognised the voice. What is also frustrating is that Trevor and Aaron did not get to see this lineup, and neither did any of the victims from the Paynesville attacks.

This same day, the examination results come from Danny's vehicle and match the crime scene tracks. The search for Jacob continues, but the FBI find a fibre that was taken from Heinrich's car, the one he owned at the time Jared was assaulted, which was a match from the fibre found on Jared's snowsuit that day.

Thankfully, Heinrich is arrested for the abduction and assault of Jared Scheierl. Heinrich was intoxicated when he was arrested, but not for long. Unfortunately, according to Gudmundson, the FBI agents who interrogated Heinrich were inexperienced. Heinrich denied any connection to the crime and said he was being framed. FBI profilers who observe the interrogation don't seem to file a report but reportedly tell detectives they don't think Heinrich's guilty. Heinrich is released.[9]

The 17 February 1990 came around, which would have been Jacob's 12th birthday. This is the day the Jacob Wetterling Foundation was launched. Its focus was on the prevention and elimination of stranger abductions of children. $200,000 was raised at the time of this launch. More and more time passes and leads still come in, but nothing is fruitful. And then came 22 October 1990, a year after Jacob's disappearance, but they were still no closer to finding him.

Then, in early 1991, a Paynesville officer noticed a vehicle that seemed to be following paper boys while on their routes. The officer observes the car and sees the man driving. At this point, the Paynesville police department is very familiar with Danny Heinrich, and lo and behold, guess who was behind the wheel? Danny Heinrich. But because he hasn't done anything illegal, the officer just lets it go.

Then, the next month, in the Paynesville paper, there was a heading that told people to be extra alert as there had been three calls to the police about a suspicious man spotted by children in the area and that this man would watch children and try and approach them. The article says that the man is of medium build and drives a blue car. Who do we know that goes a blue car? Danny Heinrich.

In March 1990, investigators interviewed a man named Duane Hart, a known sex offender who was in prison at the time. Hart was previously interviewed as a person of interest in Jacob's abduction, but it was believed he had nothing to do with it. Funnily enough, Jared was aware of Duane Hart and wanted to meet him to hear his voice so he could determine if this was the man who assaulted him or if he was still out there. However, he was not allowed to talk to him.

Coincidentally, Hart was a friend of Danny's older brother, and he and Danny would hang out occasionally. He was around sixteen years older than Danny, and allegedly, they had partaken in sexual intercourse. Hart says he was at Danny's apartment the month Jacob was abducted, and while he was there, he saw two police scanners, a handgun and a ninja-type suit. Hart says Heinrich even asked him how to get rid of a body. You would think after this, the police would actively look into Danny Heinrich more, but no. Hart even tells them he thinks Heinrich took Jacob, but no follow-up was done.

So, cases like these do what they usually do: grow cold. Around the second anniversary of Jacob's disappearance, the investigation stalled. Years passed, and there was still no sign of Jacob. People seem to forget. But not the Wetterling's. Patty became a national advocate for children, and she and Jerry founded the *Jacob Wetterling Resource Centre*, which works to help prevent child exploitation. In 1994, Jacob's parents successfully lobbied Congress to pass the *Jacob Wetterling Act*, which requires states to register sex offenders. But more years passed, and there was still no sign of Jacob.

Fast forward to 2002, a man named John Sanner was elected as the Stearns County Sheriff, and he aspired to be the one to find the man responsible for Jacob's disappearance. But first, he needed a suspect. He doesn't look at Heinrich, but he goes to Dan Rassier. The 33-year-old man who lived at the farmhouse with his parents, whose driveway began right at the spot Jacob was abducted. Occam's Razor would say they are a viable suspect, but does this equate to the amount of evidence against Heinrich?

They go to Dan and try to get him to admit that he took Jacob. Dan says that they never knew each other even though he lived less than a mile from the Wetterling's. When investigators started digging deeper, people in the community could not believe they were looking into him as a person of interest, especially since the Rassier family was a long-standing, respected family in Stearns County.

Dan was constantly harassed, mainly because he was 33, living with his parents and alone. He was seen as a suspect. Even though nothing made sense, none of the shoes matched or belonged to Dan. They had nothing to arrest him on. But they kept pressing him and letting him know they were not letting him go quickly. Again, the investigation came to a halt until 2013, when Jared Scheierl took matters into his own hands.

After his assault, Jared and his family moved to a big, idyllic piece of land. Jared settled into a routine at school. He wrestled, played football and eventually became homecoming king. He managed to live a life, but his case was still unsolved.

In 2013, after an adventure in Alaska, a return to Paynesville, a marriage and three children, Jared discovered that there had been a string of assaults during the mid to late 1980s, the Paynesville attacks. He was curious as to whether these assaults were linked to his, and so he began his investigation, searching for similarities and red flags.

He called old friends who he thought may have valuable input. He even wrote a letter to the local newspaper describing the emotional turmoil he grew with over the decades, the fear of the dark and odd sounds. The anger and the loneliness. He urged the Paynesville victims to come forward to share their stories to solve this case. He also pushed the investigators to look back into the attacks, which they do. It brings them back to Danny Heinrich. Now, the technology has advanced over the twenty-three to twenty-four years since Jared's attack, so they still have fibre from Jared's clothing on the night of his attack and hair from Danny Heinrich.

They test the two against each other and return with a match. Jared finally knows that Danny Heinrich is the man who assaulted him. However, the statute of limitations had run out, so there was no way Heinrich could be charged. But this was enough for them to get a search warrant for Heinrich's home to see if there was any other evidence, especially evidence of Jacob.

What investigators found was an abundance of child pornography, among other things, including a bin full of children's clothing.

Heinrich was finally arrested in October 2015, and there was no way he could get out this time. While he awaited his trial, he made a startling confession in August 2016, just three weeks before the trial was about to begin.

Heinrich said he wanted to make a plea deal. He would confess to abducting and assaulting not only Jared but also Jacob. In exchange for his confession, he would get a maximum of twenty years in prison.

Prosecutors said the Wetterlings were consulted and approved the plea agreement, which required Danny to give a detailed confession and tell investigators where to find Jacob.

In a packed courtroom with Patty and Jerry Wetterling, Heinrich detailed what happened on 22 October 1989. He saw Jacob, Trevor and Aaron cycling down a rural road near Jacob's Minnesota home in St Joseph. He pulled into a driveway, and when they passed him, he turned around and faced the direction of the road they would return to. Approximately twenty minutes later, they returned, and he stepped out of his car. This matched Dan Rassier's depiction of the night.

He put on his mask, reached for his revolver and proceeded onto the road. He confronted the boys and forced them to ditch their bikes. Danny asked for their name and ages. He then told them to run away and not look back, or he would shoot. During the court case, Danny is asked if Jacob said anything to him. Jared just asked him, 'What did I do wrong?'

Heinrich dragged Jacob into his car, getting back to the main road. He headed west, onto the interstate and north to Albany. From Albany, he went to Paynesville. Specifically, onto the Sewage Pond Road, about a hundred yards up, there was an approach and a field next to a grove of trees. He drove as close as he could to the grove of trees. Stopping the car, he exited and opened the door for Jacob, uncuffing him. He took him to the edge of the grove of trees and assaulted him.

Afterwards, Jacob asked him if he was going to take him home. Heinrich said he could not take him, so Jacob started to cry. At this point, Heinrich spotted a patrol car that came down the road with no siren and headed east to Paynesville. Panicked, Heinrich pulled the revolver out of his pocket, asking Jacob to turn around where he shot him.

Checking he was dead, he left his body and went home. After a couple of hours had passed, he returned to where he left him, dragging his body from the place he shot him, digging a grave with a little shovel and placing him in. He camouflaged the area with grass and walked back home, throwing Jacob's tennis shoes into a ravine another 100 yards down the road just because he forgot to bury them with him.

Danny returned to the burial site a year later, digging up his remains, placing his jacket, his bones and his skull into a bag to move it. Transferring the remains onto a nearby farm into another hole.

On 31 August 2016, he showed law enforcement the site where he buried Jacob's remains the second time. Heinrich then also admits to acting alone in the kidnap, sexual assault and murder of Jacob. After discussing what happened to Jacob, they turned to Jared Scheierl and what happened to him. Heinrich admitted to abducting and sexually assaulting Jared on 13 January 1989.

Jacob's clothing and human remains were unearthed from a pasture near Paynesville, about 30 miles (48 km) away from the Wetterling home and the abduction site and a short distance from where Heinrich was living in 1989. On 3 September, the remains were confirmed through dental records to be Jacob's. His mother, Patty Wetterling, told television station KARE11, a local NBC affiliate, that the remains found were indeed Jacob's. She said: 'All I can confirm is that Jacob has been found, and our hearts are broken. I am not responding to any media yet as I have no words.' The family was most likely praying that Jacob would return to them alive.[10]

Additionally, in the plea agreement, Heinrich agreed to plead guilty to one count of the twenty-five federal child pornography charges brought against him.

In exchange for Heinrich's plea, the prosecutors agreed not to charge him with Wetterling's murder. Following the plea agreement, Heinrich was sentenced to the maximum prison term of 20 years for the child pornography charge. In addition, the plea deal will allow state authorities to seek his civil commitment as a sexual predator at the end of his federal prison term, which could prevent him from ever going free.

In January 2017, Heinrich was transferred to Federal Medical Centre, Devens, a federal prison in Massachusetts, to serve his twenty-year sentence.

Jared Scheierl helped solve a decade-long mystery, providing himself and the Wetterling family closure, something investigators could not do. Occam's Razor could have worked if the investigation had not been mishandled. If investigators had looked at the surmountable evidence they had uncovered, the tyre tracks, for example, they could have solved this case.

Don Gudmundson knew this, and in September 2016, he delivered a brutal assessment of the cascading errors of the investigation. The occasion drew eight people and twenty news cameras to a packed basement room in the Stearns County Sheriff's Office, and it was the release of the state's 787-page investigative file. Gudmundson described multiple points early in the Wetterling investigation where it was clear Heinrich should have been the prime suspect but that basic errors in policing allowed him to elude justice as crucial evidence and tips went unnoticed or unattended. He was scathing and candid.

He detailed several leads that were overlooked, and that would have connected the Wetterling case to similar crimes in the area, including the kidnapping of 12-year-old Jared Scheierl in early 1989 and a series of attacks on young boys in nearby Paynesville. He said authorities received a tip less than 48 hours after Wetterling was abducted from a boy who'd been attacked by a man in Paynesville who used the same "quick, military, and proficient" style as Jacob's abductor. Yet it took investigators nearly three months to follow up on this lead.

It was a mess of epic proportions. It can be argued that if Occam's Razor had been applied and investigators looked at the leads they were given and the geographical radius the attacks were centred upon, Heinrich could have been arrested earlier. Actual survivors would not have been forgotten by law enforcement and forced to take matters into their own hands. Gudmundson said it best; 'there was a lot of manpower; most of it was squandered.' He also described Heinrich. 'When Heinrich comes, because the case is so big, they're so overwhelmed, it was like a whisper in the crowd. But you know what it should have been? A persistent whisper.'[11]

I think the best way to end this case is to quote Patty Wetterling. A day before Heinrich's trial, she wrote a brief message on the *Jacob Wetterling Resource Page*.

'Everyone wants to know what they can do to help us. Say a prayer, light a candle, be with friends, play with your children, giggle, hold hands, eat ice cream, create joy and help your neighbour. This is what will bring me comfort today.'[12]

Chapter Six

The Body in Room 348

On 16 September 2010, Susie Fleniken was pacing anxiously around her room. The day prior, her husband, Greg Fleniken, checked into Room 348 of the MCM Elegante Hotel in Beaumont, Texas.[1] They had emailed about Susie's progress on a computer program to file for a tax extension. He said, 'You're doin' good babe.' They were the type of couple who spoke every morning, catching up on the day before.

But she had not heard from him since.

Susie kept trying his mobile ineffectively. She called Greg's colleagues, who revealed that Greg had not turned up for work that was not like him. So, two of his co-workers drove to the hotel and knocked on his door.

There was no answer. Concern was building, so they got the hotel manager to open the door. They were hit with an instant heat. Room 348 was stuffy and hot, and that is where they found Greg.

Greg Fleniken was dead on the floor, bent forward with his face pressed to the carpet. There was a slight wet spot on his pyjamas near the crotch, which was not unusual. A burned cigarette was neatly tucked between the fingers of his left hand. His skin colour had turned a greyish blue.

The co-workers and hotel manager were aghast in that warm room, gazing in disbelief at his body.

Greg Fleniken was a 55-year-old man who was very set in his ways. He liked his routines. He was a Landman for the company he co-owned with his brother, dealing with mineral rights on private property in a thriving oil-land leading business based in a small city east of Houston.

Every Monday morning, Greg would make the two-hour drive in his pickup from Lafayette, Louisiana, heading west on Interstate Ten through farmland fragmented only by oil derricks, cell phone towers, 'adult' superstores and billboards. He spent a lot of time on the road, which comes with the territory. He travelled light and lived tidily.

After so many years on the road, he would leave his rolling suitcase open on the floor of his hotel room and use it as a drawer. Dirty clothes went on the closet floor. Shirts he wanted to use and keep uncreased hung above. Toiletries were in the pockets of a cloth folding case that hooked onto the towel rack in the bathroom.

At the end of every day, he would slide off his worn brown leather boots and line them up by the suitcase, drop his faded jeans to the floor, and put on lightweight cotton pyjama bottoms.

Most evenings, he never left the room. He wasn't afraid of his own company and was used to solitary nights as part of his work.

The hotel Greg frequented was just off the Cloverleaf outside Beaumont. His company rented a room in the 'Cabana,' a three-story wing wrapped around a small swimming pool and framed by potted palms.

Greg's long-standing routine was watching TV while he smoked cigarettes and ate candy bars. His poison for that evening was a Reese's Crispy Crunchy bar alongside his Root Beer. The heat was stifling in Texas, so Greg turned the air conditioner all the way up. He had his feet up and was watching Iron Man 2. Unfortunately, he wouldn't see Iron Man win.

At some point during the end of the film, amid the artificial violence and computer-generated graphics, Greg is struck with a real and staggering blow. A blow so violent it would blind a man in pain. He managed to get off the bed and move towards the door before gravity overcame him, and he fell, legs splayed and face first. He was most likely dead by the time his face hit the rug.

The hotel manager and co-workers' distress calls brought an ambulance and the Beaumont Police, along with Detective Scott Apple, who showed up a little more than an hour and a half later. Scott Apple can be depicted as a man who was *all cop*. He lived and breathed his work, and his wife worked in the same field. However, he looked at the scene before him and saw little to pique his interest.

There was no sign of a break-in or struggle. Everything in the room was in its place. The only thing out of place was Greg's body on the ground. His wallet was still in the back pocket of his jeans, inside a stack of $100 bills. So, robbery was not the prerogative.

Those residing in neighbouring rooms heard nothing out of the ordinary. As Apple interviewed the neighbours, he rapidly concluded that this was probably a 'natural causes thing.'[2]

Apple investigated Greg's bag, looking for pills, medication, and some clues to his collapse, but nothing came to fruition.

Susie and Michael later confided to Apple that Greg never went to a doctor. He was as stubborn as a mule, suspicious of authority and unmoved by the idea of health and fitness. He did not exercise and had chain-smoked his entire adult life, with an unceasing cough to prove it.

Greg did not eat or drink excessively, but he did both freely, and it became elementary to conclude that his death was due to his lifestyle choices catching up with him. Occam's Razor would concur and say case closed. Even Susie was ready to believe it. She was evidently shocked and grief-stricken, but she almost wanted to accept that that was the cause of her husband's death just for the sake of closure. At least he checked out on his own terms, so to speak.

But we have learned from these cases that nothing is ever simple, and neither is Greg's death.

The police saw the death as routine, unremarkable. A photographer snapped photos to make a record of the scene, and the body was taken to the Jefferson County Medical Examiner for an autopsy. The only mystery here was the cause of death, and this was likely only a minor mystery if that.

Dr Tommy Brown, the man performing the autopsy, was all business, crisp, efficient and confident. He had a proven method; it took him forty-five minutes to conduct a post-mortem examination, inspecting a body inside and out. He did everything fast. He even spoke quickly. And as a loyal, respected member of the legal landscape of Jefferson County, his word was law.

He examined Greg's body, and the circumstance was mundane at the forefront, but what was on the table was anything but. The 55-year-old was in decent shape. After methodical inspection, the only marks Brown found on his body was the one-inch abrasion on Greg's cheek, more than likely from when his face hit the ground. Curiously, there was a half-inch laceration on Greg's scrotum.

Upon further inspection, the sack was swollen and discoloured, with a small amount of oedema fluid framing the wound. The bruising had spread through the groin area and across the right. Something had hit him *hard*.

The tale his body spun grew more intriguing. When Brown opened the front of Greg's torso, he discovered an astonishing amount of blood and extensive internal damage. A small amount of partly digested food had been torn from his intestines. Brown uncovered further lacerations there and on his stomach liver, as well as two broken ribs and a hole in the right atrium of his heart.

The disquieting condition on his internals reflected severe trauma. It looked like Greg had been beaten or crushed to death. Brown concluded that the wound to his genitals had been caused by a hard kick. He had also taken a blow to the chest so severe that it had caused lethal damage. He would have bled out in thirty seconds or less. So, dying from natural causes? Evidently not. On the official form, in the section, 'Manner of Death', Brown wrote, 'Homicide.'

In disbelief, Apple called Brown to explain this shut case be forced back open. He listened, flabbergasted, as Brown detailed Greg's internal injuries being equivalent to that of crash victims or someone found crushed under a heavy object.

There were not many murders in Beaumont. Greg's being one in ten of that year was about the average.

Yet, the physical evidence does not add up to how Greg was found. Unless he was beaten to death elsewhere, taken and placed back in his room. But how does a man get beaten so grievously that his ribs crack, his heart ruptures, and his inner organs tear, while his torso doesn't have as much as a dent? And how could any of this have occurred without anyone in adjacent rooms hearing a thing? Nothing about this made sense.

Can we even answer why? Why was Greg Fleniken killed? He appeared to have no enemies. Susie was in her 20s when she met Greg and adored him. So much so that she married him twice. Once when they were in their 20s, until they separated for several years, and again when they reconciled in middle age.

When Susie called him again after the separation, he said, 'I've been waiting for you to call.' They had been married for another fifteen years.

Greg's brother and co-workers confirmed that the company universally liked him, and his frequentation at the Elegante rarely intervened in anyone's life. He kept himself to himself, never going to the bar, socialising, drinking or picking up any women. So, he wasn't a man who got himself in sticky, potentially murderous situations. This was a decent, honourable man who people liked. Not the sort of man someone would go out of their way to murder. But someone had.

And Apple needed to find out who. Fall melted into winter in 2010 as Apple pursued many possibilities. Maintenance records showed that at some point early in the evening of his death, Greg was cooking pre-packed popcorn in the microwave and had fortuitously blown an electrical circuit. The outage affected the adjacent room, 349 and the rooms directly underneath. Greg called the front desk to report the outage and confessed his role abashedly to the maintenance man who came up to reset the breaker.

This led to two theories.

One involved, as it usually always does, sex. The Elegante maintenance man happened to have a record as a sex offender. Apple thought maybe the puncture wound to the scrotum and internal injuries had been caused by a long screwdriver. Some sort of assault imitating penetration. Apple spent a lot of time talking to the maintenance man and looking into his background, but this theory remained true: a theory that never advanced suspicion.

The second theory involved a group of union electricians staying at the same hotel who had been in room 349 when Greg died. They were in town for an extended stay, working for an oil company. They tended to gather in one another's rooms for a drink at night. Apple theorised that maybe they had been drinking heavily, were irritated by the accidental power outage, and had had an altercation with Greg. Maybe they assaulted him in the hallway. Could Greg, badly beaten, have returned to his room and then collapsed? Some of the electricians had been questioned the day Greg's body was found but confirmed that they had not had any interaction with him. Furthermore, this doesn't match the fact that Greg's body was unbruised.

Nine days after Greg's death, with a colleague, Apple interviewed the electricians again, this time with a hidden video camera. The men they encountered, Lance Mueller and Tim Steinmetz, who resided in room 349, were appropriately curious and friendly. However, they did not share anything substantial. They thought they had heard the man in the next room coughing when they returned from the bar. They were just as confused as Apple about his death; however, they did not think he had been crushed because there was nothing heavy enough in the room to warrant it.

They found three more electricians down the hall: Trent Pasano, Thomas Elkins and Scott Hamilton. They were friendly and endeavoured to be helpful. One confirmed that when he saw the body on the gurney in the elevator, he had assumed they were caterers delivering a cake or big food tray.

Pasano corroborated that he had been in the room with Mueller and Steinmetz that night but hadn't seen anything. The alibi seemed pretty solid.

The electricians handed over their licences gave Apple their phone numbers, and helpfully stated that they would be in town for a few months, and if anything came up, they were more than happy to assist.

Weeks go by, and then months.

Apple worked any theory he could imagine: Susie had her husband killed, Michael, killing him, but there was nothing that hinted at either person being the culprit. His theories were inefficacious. The matter of Greg Fleniken and the body found in room 348 was bound for the cold files, just another sad box of notes and evidence stored in the Jefferson County Court House. But not on Susie Fleniken's watch.

Susie took matters into her own hands and brought in Ken Brennan.

Ken Brennan took Susie's phone call while on a golf course. She was shocked that he picked up the phone himself. 'Oh, my God, you don't have a secretary?'[3] She was flustered and could barely get the story of Greg's death, the coroners' findings and the dead end out of her mouth.

In his thick New York accent, Brennan asked her to send files and as much information as possible, and he would take a look, but not before endearing Susie to take care of herself; he was a lovely man like that.

A former Long Island cop and D.E.A Special Agent, Brennan made a good living as a private detective in Florida.

He is easily found on the internet and is often sent more cases than he can handle. People come to him with unsolved murders and disappearances. He takes these cases seriously and holds them gently. When he scours a file, he looks for a case that intrigues him and where he can do something meaningful. He says he 'ain't in the business of giving people false hopes.'

Greg's case piqued his interest because of the mystery and because he saw so many avenues to explore – hotel guests, the maintenance man, and even Greg's co-workers and family. To Apple, none of these leads were deemed fresh anymore, but to Brennan, they were full of promise.

Brennen paid Lafayette a visit in April, where he investigated Susie first, asking her tough questions about Greg, their relationship, his faithfulness and insurance arrangements until he was satisfied that she would have no apparent motive to have him killed. He asked her one final question; 'was there anything about the crime scene that didn't seem right to you?' Susie told him she was surprised the room was so warm because Greg liked to crank up the A.C. at night.

Satisfied, Brennan went home and arranged a second trip to Beaumont. Apple met him late at a sports bar, and the two men ate and talked. Brennan wanted to assure Apple that he wouldn't botch up his case, but he was also reading him. In the end, he came to the conclusion that he liked him.

The following morning, Apple picked Brennan up, and they visited the hotel room. Apple showed him the crime scene photos and the autopsy results, reviewing what he had done over the previous seven months. Brennan heard him out and then announced that he knew how Greg died, when, and who killed him and that he was going to catch him.

To be sure, he called Susie, asking if Greg was left or right-handed and what his favoured hand was to hold his cigarette. He was right-handed, and he always smoked with his right hand.

Brennan concluded that since Susie had already told him how cold Greg kept his room, this helped fix the time of death. In Brennan's eyes, the air conditioner had shut down everything else when the circuit breaker blew, and hotel records showed that their repairman had left Greg alive and well around 8.30 pm.

Iron Man 2 resumed, and apparently, Greg forgot to turn the A.C. back on. It would have taken a few minutes for the room to warm up enough for him to notice, and by the time it had, he was dead.

The cigarette scorched the notion that Greg had been beaten severely somewhere else, even just out in the hall, and then returned to 348. Whilst a hallway scenario might explain why nothing had been disturbed in the room, the cigarette ruled that out. There was no way Greg's attacker would have added the touch of cupping one hand under his body and delicately placing a burning cigarette between his fingers. It was also unlikely that, given the ruptured atrium, Greg would have had time to wander back into the room after a beating and calmly lit a cigarette before dying. He likely lit the cigarette before whatever happened to him had the chance to occur. The cigarette was in his left hand because Greg had gotten up from the bed and headed toward the door, shifting the cigarette to his left hand to grab the door handle with his right.

He knew a lot did not make sense to start, but Brennan was an expert in patience. A crime was a puzzle; if even one small piece did not fit, the puzzle was incomplete, so he was willing to follow the evidence in unlikely directions. Even when the conclusions it suggested were absurd. We know Occam's Razor eliminates theories that are impenetrable and hard to prove and disprove but allows us to make conclusions with limited insights or information. Could we suggest that that is what Brennan is doing here? Drawing conclusions with limited information?

Greg could not have been beaten to death in his room, as the evidence suggested, but he died there quickly after sustaining his wounds. Brennan was convinced that Greg had been minding his own business before he was killed.

The next port of call to investigate? The electricians. The blown circuit had partly blacked out their room at the same time Greg's had been. So, of all the scenarios Apple has considered, that was the one that made the most sense. The electricians may have been inebriated, may have confronted Greg in the doorway, exchanged some words and kicked him to death right there. Brennan asked Apple if he had interviewed them, and he said yes, they were friendly, and he did not notice anything unusual. But Brennan believed they were still an avenue that needed to be crossed. So they paid a visit to Dr Brown.

Brennan wanted to know if the trauma within Greg's body could have been caused by a severe beating. Brown confirmed it might have, and the scrotum laceration could have been caused by a hard kick, especially if the assailant had been wearing steel-toed boots. The electricians next door wore construction boots, and Occam's Razor would rule in favour.

Coming up with a game plan, Brennan asked Apple to begin interviewing the men who worked with the union electricians that previous summer. At the same time, he returned home to continue inspecting the hotel's surveillance video. It was an onerous task and not the most obliging.

He watched footage of Greg coming in from work that evening and several electricians making trips to their vehicles in the parking lot, but nothing worth scepticism.

When Brennan returned to Beaumont in late May, he and Apple went to see some of the co-workers that had not yet been interviewed, as Apple's efforts had uncovered nothing notable. By this point, the union electricians had been gone for seven months, but Brennan was still convinced that something was there. If any one of the electricians knew something about Greg's death, information would have spread amongst them like a circle of Chinese Whispers.

They made the rounds and mainly got the same inane answers: the electricians knew about the murder, and they thought it was such a shame, but that was it. Until one of the foremen, Aaron Bourque heard something about a gun going off in a boarding house.

Apple was fast to correct Aaron; that gunshot was not the same case. That was when a man got into a fight at the Elegante Hotel. But alarm bells were ringing in Brennan's head. This was the first he had heard about a fight at the Elegante Hotel or gunshots.

Brennan was adamant that they needed to go back to the hotel. He wanted to look for a bullet.

Back where this case began in room 348, they began scrutinizing the floor, the furniture, the walls, everything. Working on their hands and knees, shining flashlights under furniture, but they found nothing. The frustration was apparent on Brennan's face because he was convinced a gun was involved, and he was determined to find evidence of it. But he was about to call this a losing battle until he noticed an indention in the wall alongside the closed door that led into the adjourning room. A repair job. It appeared to be right where the handle of the door would hit the wall, but when he swung the door open, the knob and the dent didn't quite match. In fact, the doorknob touched the wall slightly to the right.

Brennan asked the security guy to let them into room 349 on a hunch, and there was no mistaking what they found there. A small, neat hole in the wall had been patched with a daub of faintly pink filler that turned out to be dried toothpaste. Measuring its height against his hip, Brennan walked back into 348 and measured the indention on that side. *They lined up.*

Beaumont's crime scene investigators carefully excavated both holes and shined a laser through. The trajectory pointed straight up to the bed where Greg had been sitting and watching his movie.

He had been shot.

Dr Brown needed more convincing. He did not believe that his method as coroner could have missed a bullet wound. And to bring Greg's killer to justice, Brennan and Apple knew they needed Brown to rewrite his findings. You could not argue in court that a defendant had shot someone if the medical examiner's office had concluded that the victim hadn't been. But Brown refused to have the body exhumed; it was expensive and disturbing to the family. In this case, it was impossible because Greg had been cremated. The ovens were not enough to destroy metal fragments.

But Brennan was a people person. He knew how to work Brown. He asked him to humour him and take out the autopsy photos to see what they could find.

Brown indulged him, and they looked at the photographs, passing them back and forth across the desk.

In Brennan's mind, he knew what he was looking at. He knew the bullet had entered Greg's scrotum and torn up through him. The skin of the scrotum was soft and pliable, and it had folded over the entry wound, making it less obvious what it was. The internal injuries traced the bullet's fatal trajectory. He asked Brown if it was a possibility that this extensive damage could have been done by a bullet, which Brown concurred, but he was convinced that this man had been beaten.

Finally, they looked at a photo of the heart, and that's when Brennan found his golden ticket. The bullet hole.

Brown explained that sometimes when a man is kicked or hit with a blunt object in the chest, it is the right atrium that usually bursts.

Brown looked at the bullet hole, almost resigned. After a long moment, he said, 'The media is going to kill me on this.'

Now, it was time for Brennan and Apple to look at where the bullet came from. They go straight for Tim Steinmetz.

Steinmetz met the detectives in an interview room at the Chippewa County Sheriff's Department; he was surprised that they had come all the way to Wisconsin to meet him, especially considering it had been more than seven months. He wasn't apprehensive, however, because they could not have been nicer. He also wasn't apprehensive because he had already corroborated his story with Lance Mueller. If that doesn't scream suspicious, I don't know what does.

Tim sat in a swivel chair on one side of a big wooden table, and they sat opposite him with their notebooks open and files handy. They thanked him for coming in, assured him that this was routine and walked him through the evening, asking many questions, with Steinmetz answering diligently, trying to remember every detail. He confirmed that he didn't hear any commotion from Greg's room, nothing out of the ordinary. Brennan and Apple took notes diligently, asking Steinmetz to review the declaration and statement.

He was confused. Did they come all the way out here for this?

As instructed by Brennan, Steinmetz read the declaration out loud and made any necessary changes. Steinmetz altered 'apprentice' to 'journeyman', a few minor things. Every place he made a change, he signed. A local police officer came in to notarize the statement in his presence, and Steinmetz thought he was free at home. Until Brennan's harsh voice travelled across to him.

'Now you've got a problem.'

Brennan was adamant that Steinmetz had signed a false statement; this was an offence, and so he threatened jail time, in particular, jail time with Lance Mueller. Apple played the good cop to Brennen's bad, gently coercing Steinmetz to give in, to tell the truth. And he did; it all came gushing out of Steinmetz's mouth.

Later on 1 June 2011, Trent Pasano, who had been in 349 with them, confirmed his account in an interview. There was a pattern between the two accounts, and it was as follows: the pair had been drinking beer. Mueller asked Pasano to fetch his 9-mm Ruger pistol and a bottle of whisky from his car. When Pasano came back, Mueller pulled out the revolver and, to the alarm of the others, began fiddling with it. When it went off, he aimed it at Pasano at the foot of the bed, and Steinmetz, who tumbled to the floor, cursed at him. Pasano momentarily believed he had been struck before turning to discover a hole in the wall.

Mueller panicked, they both said. Mueller packed up the rifle and took it back out to his car. Pasano had departed for his own room when he came back, disgusted. Steinmetz and Mueller proceeded to the bar downstairs.

Steinmetz claimed that until they heard someone in the room coughing extremely late, after midnight, when they returned from the bar, they had no way of knowing if anyone was staying next door.

He did not hide anything. The entire situation was outlined in Steinmetz's second and most honest statement. It was cathartic, getting things off his chest. He told Brennan that he and Mueller were disturbed when they saw the cops in room 348 the following morning and the gurney. 'I believed he had murdered that man.'

The only element that didn't make sense was the cough from behind 348's door, heard when the two returned from the bar. Brennan and Apple were unwilling to give it much weight for several reasons. If it were accurate, Greg would have survived the gunshot for a lot longer than the coroner had anticipated, but it would not have changed the death's cause. It made the electricians' disregard for his well-being and reluctance to seek assistance all the more shocking. It's more likely they had heard Greg sneezing in the space the day before. They had been in the room next to him that night, too.

Brennan asked him if he checked on Greg, and Steinmetz said no, that will always be a big 'what if' for him. Brennan and Apple may have gotten a confession, but there is one last thing they wanted Steinmetz to do for them. Call Mueller. Apple and Brennan were recording the conversation. He told Mueller the truth, that they had caught his lie, and that Apple and Brennan got the truth out of him. Steinmetz suggested that Mueller call Apple right away.

But Mueller was stubborn; he refused to believe the detectives knew the truth. Over the subsequent minutes of the call, he circled Steinmetz repeatedly. The man had not passed away from a gunshot wound, according to the postmortem report his lawyer had gotten. The news has covered the incident extensively.

The autopsy findings supported Mueller's contention that the guy in 348's death and the unintentional shooting were unrelated. Mueller had convinced himself with every fibre of his being that it had nothing to do with him.

The guilt must have eaten at him because a few hours later. Brennan got a call from none other than Mueller, who was definitely a couple of beers deep. He wanted to explain himself and make a statement. But Brennan cooly suggested that he should call his attorney.

Fast forward to 29 October 2012, Ken Brennan had flown to Beaumont to join Susie Fleniken, Scott Apple and a cohort of Greg's family and friends for the sentencing of Lance Mueller. The electrician had entered a no-contest plea to manslaughter. As Brennan remembered it, the judge began by saying that this tragedy might be considered a terrible accident. The inexorability of unfortunate discoveries.

Brennan panicked here, thinking this guy would only be sentenced for a year, but the judge pulled through and began cataloguing the long list of wilfully irresponsible choices that had led to this day.

Mueller was sentenced to 10 years, which is only half of what the law allows. No matter how earnest, Mueller's court apology came too late. He made the criminally negligent choice to play with a gun while intoxicated. They had known from the beginning, as Steinmetz had stated, that the stray bullet had, at the very least, contributed to the death of the man in room 348. The bullet may have even caused a heart attack, which was the initial theory when the police rolled his body out on a trolley. Nevertheless, once the coroner determined that Greg had suffered blunt-force trauma and died, Mueller was glad to accept the possibility that Greg had been killed by anything, even though it was difficult to envision what.

He had, though, had enough anxiety over the gunshot. He had personally used toothpaste to repair the hole. He promptly hid the weapon in his car, kept it with a buddy for a few days following the incident, and then turned it over to a lawyer for safekeeping before leaving Texas. There was a blatant disregard for life here, a life Greg had and a disregard for those who were impacted by Greg's death. In particular, his wife, Susie.

Susie Fleniken had a chance to speak to Mueller directly in the courtroom that day. She had waited two years to look at her husband's murderer, eye to eye. 'You have met your match,' said the small woman, staring across the courtroom at him, a study in controlled ferocity. 'I would have spent the rest of my life tracking you down. And I found you. Greg's murderer. I brought you to justice.'

The case of the body in room 348 is fantastic because I could read anthologies of Ken Brennan's exploits and not get tired of them. I would devour a Netflix series about the cases he helped solve. But this case, in particular, was also fantastic because you can tell how the investigators, such as Apple, wanted Occam's Razor to work so badly.

Greg's room wasn't damaged or broken into, and Greg was likeable in a happy marriage with no enemies. There was no damage or trauma to his external body. Crudely, you had to look deeper into the case, as the coroner had to look deeper into Greg's body to see if something was amiss.

This case is serendipitous since true crime cannot ever be simple. The idea of correlating simplicity with true crime is ludicrous because the theory that a bullet could have hit someone in the scrotum and killed them would not have been the first hypothesis to investigate. Especially if the coroner missed the bullet hole in the body in the first place. And if the bullet hole in the room was hurriedly covered up with toothpaste.

If you look at Occam's Razor as a rule of thumb and use it to test multiple hypotheses, then maybe the electricians next door would have been focused on. Still, it took verging away from simple explanations and probabilities to really come to grips with what happened to Greg. If

Susie Fleniken hadn't persisted, and if Brennan and Apple hadn't looked deeper, there may not have been any closure, and Greg Fleniken's case would have gathered dust in the corner with other cold cases.

Chapter Seven

The Strange Disappearance of Jerika Binks

On 18 February 2018, the fifty-two-degree weather in American Fork, Utah, enticed Jerika Alvery Binks, 24, to go for a run. Jerika was an avid runner. She would go on thirty-mile runs at once and aspired to complete a hundred-mile run.

The day's warmth would slowly seep into a haze of snow clouds that congregated over the Wasatch Mountains, looming above the city from the east. By the next morning, a blizzard would white out the town, and another mystery would be brewing. The weather was a precursor for the events that followed.

Jerika is the second oldest of four. Her mother had second siblings who had kids that Jerika grew up with, a large, close-knit family.[1] She could light up a room every time she walked into it and always gave great hugs. Quick-witted and fun to be around with a personality akin to her favourite personality from *Jersey Shore*, Pauly D. She would go around the house saying, 'Yeah, buddy!'

That fateful day in February, Jerika had been planning on running with her roommate, but her roommate decided to frequent church instead that Sunday. This wasn't a dealbreaker for Jerika, who loved the outdoors and frequently ran alone. She also took self-defence classes and went duck hunting with her 20-year-old brother, Porter. She dreamed of opening her own gym someday, and her mother, Suzanne Westring, described her as 'pure muscle.'

9.00 am hit, and Jerika put on her new running shoes, a pair of dark green leggings with a two-tone grey hoodie. She left her wallet and ID at home because she didn't need them, but she grabbed her other essentials: her phone, water bottle, and earbuds. She often listened to country music to set her pace but had lately been fixated on a Pandora pop workout station suggested by her sister, Sydney, aged 22.

Jerika didn't use a tracker, running app or Apple watch, but at 9.30 am, she turned left onto North County Boulevard, a busy street framed with chains like Dollar Tree and McDonald's and ranch-style houses. Surveillance footage chartered her path past the Mormon Temple, where birthday parties would gather for photos in the garden outside, and patches of lollipop-coloured tulips would sprout in the spring.[2]

Jerika was recorded jogging steadily past the Utah State Developmental Centre at 9.38 am, then at 9.50 am, past a Walmart where she was known to buy her everyday groceries. From there, she headed east towards the snow-capped mountains and American Fork Canyon, a wooded paradise of trails popular with hikers and rock climbers.

At this point, she was clocking a pace of a mile every nine minutes, according to surveillance. She reached the entrance to the Highland Trail at 9.55 am. This route would wind her through scenic parts of the canyon, the mountain goats, and fir trees fit for Christmas. This was supposed to be the peaceful part of her run, *but Jerika never made it out.*

Jogging is not supposed to be dangerous, but if you are a woman, there are always additional dangers you must look for. That shadow in the corner, the stares as you run, the apprehensive and jumpy feeling, it's never ever a peaceful run. In one survey in 2017, one-third of female joggers reported having been followed by someone in a vehicle, bicycle or by foot, and nearly half reported experiencing harassment.[3]

Stories of women being attacked while running have always dominated the news. In July of 2018, Mollie Tibbets, aged 20, went missing in Brooklyn, Iowa. A suspect was discovered from security footage after his car was seen driving back and forth. He had been following Mollie and parked, beginning to run beside her. After she rejected his advances, he claimed he lost control, his fury taking over, and he blacked out. He later found her in his trunk. On Wednesday, 12 January, 23-year-old primary school teacher Ashling Murphy was violently killed while jogging along a canal at 4.00 pm in County Offaly, Ireland.

Violence against women is a public emergency that shows no signs of abating. It is no wonder that 73% of women, me included, say they will only run if they have their phones. And 60% will only run in daylight. It is infuriating to know that women must constantly stay vigilant just to exist. Brands rush to create products that help women protect themselves, like Go Guarded, which makes a $14 ring that doubles as a sharp weapon, but when are we going to stop women from being murdered full stop? When are we going to put methods into place to stop violence against women rather than create temporary measures?

Jerika didn't have any products to help protect herself. She trusted the area she had lived in for more than a decade. In this area, it's usual to see the title 'Utah Valley University Continues Its Jazz Jam Series' in newspapers. Jerika had run countless times through this community, past apple orchards and waving walkers, and up into canyon trails reminiscent of those she had used to explore with her mother and siblings as a child. That's why she may not have been wearing a ring that may be used as a weapon. Instead, she wore a green stone band she'd bought with Sydney at the mall, the sole item missing from her jewellery box.

It's time to talk about Jerika herself. That February, Jerika's life had been on the up. When she left for her run that day, it was from a voluntary, sober living facility where she'd been residing for four months since October. Jerika had struggled with drug addiction in the past, but her family knew she was clean and committed to rebuilding her life and their trust.

Searches of her phone records coincided with that belief, as she had not been in contact with anyone from her past that could trigger her addiction. She had just started a new office job at a construction company and had saved up for a little black Mazda. Jerika had also made plans to go car shopping with her mum and 28-year-old brother, Jed, later in the week. Long story short, she had a future and present she aspired to and was creating. There would be no reason to leave it willingly.

The night before Jerika disappeared, she had gone bowling with her roommates and called her mom when she got home. There was not an inkling of anything wrong in her voice.

When Jerika did not return to the sober living facility by the next morning, a concerned employee called her mother, who lived nearby. Immediately worried, Suzanna, Jerika's mother, searched her daughters' room. This turned up all her belongings, including two uncashed checks on her desk and her wallet and ID. This disputes the idea that she had fallen off the wagon or had run away because who runs away with their wallet or any possible funds like the uncashed checks? Calls to Jerika's phone immediately went to voicemail. It didn't take a detective to realise something wasn't right here.

Suzanne was proactive and reported Jerika missing the same day, but as darkness fell, the snow did too and with it came car accidents – 217 over 12 hours – which kept all the emergency responders in the area busy. Conditions were slippery in the canyon, making searching for Jerika impossible and dangerous.

As if things couldn't get any worse, the missing person's report Suzanne made had been filed to the wrong district due to a police error, meaning no immediate action could have been made. 'We lost really crucial time in the beginning,' Suzanne says. When search crews finally set out to look for Jerika, *eight days had passed.*

The crews first focused on the preliminary mobile phone pings from Jerika's phone. One was recorded at 10.30 am at the opening of American Fork Canyon, and another at 1.30 am from a tower in Saratoga Springs ten miles away. These efforts were for naught. Three weeks later, when more accurate mobile phone data was obtained, it showed that crews had been focusing on the wrong area, as pings do not always go to the closest tower. So, they refocused their search on the canyon ever since.

Police were taking statements from potential witnesses and hikers who were in the canyon the day Jerika went missing. Brittany Lisenby, a 31-year-old photographer, had been hiking in the canyon with her boyfriend and dogs, and she reported to the police that she had heard gunshots that day. This isn't unheard of; they are in America, after all. But Lisenby stated it wasn't hunting season and sounded more like a handgun than a rifle. The noise scared her dogs, and she already felt jittery because she had passed a camp that 'looked like someone had done some sort of ritual there.' She'd seen sticks sharpened into spears placed into symbols along the ground. Which, as we have seen previously with the likes of Jane Britton, are never a good sign.

Surprisingly, Brittany's sinister tip did not result in any concrete leads. Still, for a short period, she became preoccupied with reaching out to anyone who had posted on Instagram from the Canyon on 18 February.

Did you hear the gunshots, too? These days, she refuses to go hiking without her dogs.

Weeks went by, and there was no movement in the investigation and no sign of Jerika, so Paul Conover, Jerika's uncle, started going door to door along her running route to see if anyone had seen anything or had any video footage that might offer an inclination to where she may have gone. Desperate to keep the momentum going, the family offered a $5000 reward for any information about Jerika's disappearance.

Fast forward to 28 March, as the snow melted into Little Cottonwood Creek, a break finally emerged in the case. Wildlife camera footage retrieved by park staff in the canyon showed a woman running down the Timpanogos Cave Trail at 1.30 pm. At this point, Jerika would have been outside for four hours, which was not uncommon. She would have been headed toward the road and canyon exit. The footage captures her figure from the back, wearing dark green leggings and a two-tone grey hoodie, her brown ponytail bouncing.

UCSO Detective Steve Pratt, the lead detective on the case, confirmed that the police combed through the area, searching the trail approximately three or four times for days with search and rescue, planes, helicopters and drones. They went down the shoots, across the ledges, everywhere a person could go.

Adjacent scree slopes, animal trails and other possible but unauthorised routes were also searched multiple times. The cave trail gate is locked from below but can be opened from above at all times, leaving open the possibility that she continued down the trail and left the park. Dogs searched for her scent on well-worn trails and in more remote spots. The family searched on their own, too, taking the initiative to organise four primary searches, multiple small searches and many volunteer drone flights. But there was no sign of her, none of her clothing, no water bottle, no trace of her at all.

This is where theories start to develop, and Occam's Razor comes into play again. Could Jerika have been attacked by a mountain lion? It was always possible because animals had been spotted in the area and were known to drag their victims out of sight, which would explain the lack of evidence. But mountain lions typically hunt in the morning and evening, not in the middle of the afternoon, and attacks on humans were rare anyway.

A more plausible theory could be that she slipped and fell in a remote spot of the canyon, with no way of getting in touch with anyone to help her. But that does not explain that 1.30 pm photo that shows her on a well-maintained trail approximately half a mile from the park entrance. Wouldn't a drone or helicopter have found her if she had fallen?

The second theory was that she had absconded. Earlier that year, Jerika had expressed interest in leaving the state. But again, her voluntary, sober living facility was *voluntary* - no one was keeping her there. She could have left anytime, and running away without her wallet or uncashed cheques seemed less than likely. Also, why would she flee the relationships she had worked hard to rebuild?

Jerika was known to occasionally leave the centre to meet with partners. Whether it was romantic or sexual in nature, I am not sure. Jerika used her Snapchat account to meet an individual around one week before she went missing. Still, the man was tracked down by investigators who determined that he was not involved in the case, and no further information was released.

A Facebook page was also made to spread awareness called 'Finding Jerika' in the hopes that awareness would spread and lead to her return.

In May 2018, three months after Jerika's disappearance, images captured by a wildlife camera owned by the NPS showed her running down the National Timpanogos Cave Trail and up American Fork Canyon on 18 February around 1.30 pm. So she had definitely made it to the Monument for her run.

This NPS camera was placed on the closed trail in the fall of 2017 and retrieved on 27 March 2018. The images were taken in an area closed to the public for the winter about halfway up the trail. When park staff downloaded the photos, they recognised Jerika and reported their discovery to the Utah County Sheriff's office.

Jerika's family shared photos from a trail camera that captured Jerika running on the Timpanogos Cave Trail on 18 February. This area is usually closed during the winter months. When the photos were released, the

Utah County Sheriff's Office reported that the area had already been extensively canvassed for Jerika.[4]

Jed Binks, Jerika's brother, said the family had been 'waiting for a month to release these photos. Out of respect and not wanting to step on anyone's toes who are aiding in the investigation. That's why our searches have been so dedicated to this area.'

The photos depict her coming down the trail, but there was no footage of her coming up, which leads the family to believe she gained access to the trail elsewhere and that someone showed her an entrance before her run that day.

The County Sheriff, Sergent Spencer Cannon, has a different view of the photos, as he stated that the family released the pictures without the investigators' knowledge. Cannon said that deputies believe someone in the family snapped photos with their cell phone while investigators privately showed them the pictures. The main reason the Sheriff's Office did not want the images to be released was to avoid compromising the investigation should Jerika's disappearance turn out to be a criminal matter. We seem to get two different stories from the family and the investigators. We can see the investigator's side in preserving the investigation's integrity, but does the family think they are doing enough? Let's not forget that Jerika's disappearance was logged incorrectly, losing vital time in the investigation.

Regardless of the amount of awareness they tried to raise or any discrepancies between the family and the police, nearly a year later, there was still no sign of Jerika.

Off the back of regular attacks on women, it's hard not to contemplate the idea that Jerika had been attacked. Running is a vulnerable act; you are zoned out, with headphones on, often alone, which may look like an opportunity to certain criminal men. You may be wondering why I am just saying a man could have attacked Jerika. Why can't a woman have done it? You're right. A woman could have attacked her. I assume it was a man because it's the simplest explanation. Let's be clear: I don't assume the perpetrator is male because it's the most straightforward theory, but because it's the most common cause of women who go missing and are discovered dead.

Foul play was the conclusion Suzanne came to. Even Detective Pratt admitted that abduction hadn't been ruled out.

Suzanne did not want to imagine running would be dangerous for Jerika when running was meant to be her happy place and a key agent in her recovery. It was not supposed to be the thing that caused her harm. Even though it had been a year since she went missing, Suzanne never stopped looking for her daughter.

Jerika's disappearance never went viral, which is the crudest way to put that. It was only in the small community of American Fork that people were asking questions. We saw someone like Mollie Tibbets, whose disappearance caused a wave on social media where investigators received over 2000 tips, but Jerika's case did not receive anything close to that.

Suzanne believed this lack of response to her disappearance was because of Jerika's issue with drugs. She thought it caused some people to write off her case or caused her interest to wane. This is so frustrating because, sober or not sober, people deserve to be looked for, to be considered as actual people worthy of media attention. They should not have to fit a media niche of white, pretty, good education and background to have people looking for them and for their case to be heard.

How long would parents keep looking for their child? Would they ever stop? Suzanne searched the canyon weekly and wandered aimlessly through the paths, looking for any inkling of Jerika's whereabouts, a shoe, anything. She even approached strangers to discuss the case, wondering if they could share any details that could lead to a big break. Park workers at the ticket booth would recognise her car and waive the entrance fee. She would email running groups, hoping they might remember if they saw something that day. A Utah advertising agency donated a billboard along the local interstate, reminding the public to call if they have any information about Jerika's case. Detective Pratt confirmed the case was still open, but until something new presented itself, they were not actively looking for Jerika and had no leads.

It remained this way for a year, until 14 April 2019.

On Sunday, 14 April 2019, a 70-year-old local hiker, whose name has not been released, was climbing in American Fork Canyon shortly before 8.30 pm. He was an experienced hiker who had explored the area for years but had never hiked this ravine. He noticed that the terrain was extremely rugged and steep. That is where he found shoes, clothes, a mobile phone, and *bones*.

He alerted the authorities, and the remains were recovered the next morning and transported to the Medical Examiner's office in Taylorsville. Local police announced the discovery on Monday 15 April and the remains were sent to the state medical examiner's office in Taylorsville that Monday for positive identification.

In a press conference called by the Utah County Sheriff's Office that Wednesday at 4.00 pm, county officials said that the Office of the Medical Examiner had confirmed that the remains were Jerika's.

The remains were identified through Jerika's dental records. The cause of death had not yet been determined, but officials said that Jerika suffered a severe break to her tibia and fibula, the two long bones in the lower leg. They did not believe that foul place was involved in her death, mainly because of where the remains had been found. Sergeant Cannon confirmed it would have been virtually impossible for Jerika's body to be placed in an area that remote by another individual. It was most likely that Jerika wanted to explore beyond the area's manmade paths and experienced an accidental fall. With the snowfall, she was likely beyond help when the search began.

The location of Jerika's body, in a way, explains why the search effort after her disappearance failed to find anything. Her body was located halfway up a steep ravine, away from any trails of manmade structures, around a mile northwest of the Swinging Bridge area, which is half a mile down the road from the trailhead where she was last seen.

Detective Steve Pratt hiked to where she was found and said he had to hike over two huge boulders and duck under trees. It was treacherous terrain, steep the whole way. The investigators hadn't gone that high during their search, but they didn't know where she was before getting the trial cam photos.

Investigators believe it's possible that the only two people to have been in that ravine since 18 February 2018, are Jerika Binks and the hiker who found her remains.

Following the discovery of her remains, Jerika's brother Jed spoke at a press conference about the pain of losing his sister and his memories of her. 'It hit my family just like it happened yesterday… but it was relieving too, at the same time, to know that we at least get to bring her home.

It's relieving to know that she's not somewhere doing something that's against her will, but it's still just as tough.'[5]

It's a devastating ending to this case because you can't help but hope that Jerika makes it back home to her family, who love her and who she loves so dearly. But in a way, you are almost thankful they have closure. She didn't run away, she didn't fall off the wagon, she wasn't assaulted, she was doing something she loved.

Applying Occam's Razor to the case of Jerika's disappearance – where there's no trace of her – considering the social context, as a woman, my mind gravitates toward the worst-case scenario. Especially when you link Jerika's story to Mollie Tibbets and Ashling Murphy. In a sense, Occam's Razor could have been used to wade through the quagmire of theories because if we did not bring social context into this case, the most reasonable explanation would have been that she had fallen somewhere on her run.

I believe that, nevertheless, it is essential to note that there is a culture of ignorance being nurtured, where people do not realise how women have to behave to survive. We always have to have one eye over our shoulders. We always have to have hypervigilance. We have to stay pristine and clean and cannot have any faults or flaws; otherwise, we may not have as much media coverage should we ever go missing.

Of the more than 89,000 active missing person cases at the end of 2020, 45% were people of colour, according to the FBI's National Crime Information Centre.[6] Yet only about one-fifth of missing person cases involving people of colour receive coverage, according to a 2016 analysis by criminologist Zach Sommers.[7]

We also need to think about murdered and missing indigenous women. As of 2016, the National Crime Information Centre has reported 5,712 cases of missing American Indian and Alaska Native women and girls. Strikingly, the U.S. Department of Justice's missing persons database has only reported 116 cases. The lack of communication, combined with jurisdictional issues between state, local, federal, and tribal law enforcement, makes it nearly impossible to begin the investigative process.[8]

Gender, race and patriarchy will always be intertwined. The disparities that exist between who is reported and who is neglected are too often rooted in structural racism and other inequalities.

I don't wish to take any support away from anyone's case because everyone deserves to be searched for. Still, we must consider the nuances and unequal treatment of missing persons. We need to try and change our and the media's narratives and how society thinks about the disappearance of women, girls and gender – non conforming people. We need to try and even the playing fields so everyone, regardless of their appearance, gets the awareness they need to make it back home.

It is up to us, corporations, media networks and those who hold power to create space to level the playing field so that all types of people may be heard and reflected. Only with that change may we see a difference in who and what is deemed valuable enough for reporting and potentially saving.

Jerika's family still run their Facebook page 'Finding Jerika', and they use it to spread awareness of missing people in Utah and beyond, sharing hopeful posts of people who are found. Among the pages are scattered memories, photos, and videos of Jerika expressed by those who love her. Jerika is proof that grief and mourning are the price we pay for love, but their death is not the end, and that love can always be expressed and shared.

You can look at the Facebook page if you google 'Finding Jerika.'

Chapter Eight

The Spy in the Bag

Monday 23 August 2010, around 5.00 pm, PC John Gallagher was out on foot patrol in Pimlico, right in the heart of London, encircled by garden squares regency architecture, sandwiched between Belgravia and Westminster.

The evening was pleasantly warm, the streets filled with the first wave of commuters heading home by a nearby Victoria station.

Many commuters will have come from the various government buildings, but a select few will work for the distinctive, multi-tiered building on the embankment just across Vauxhall Bridge. It resembles a futuristic Aztec temple, ostentatious despite its purpose, home to the secret intelligence service known as MI6.

Gallagher knew, despite how striking the building was with its ornate entrances and balconies, the honey-coloured façade gave little indication of what went on behind closed doors to those who work in the shadows.

He kept his pace steady and unhurried, his expression approachable but alert from years of conditioning and training when he got a call from the control room.

Gallagher was instructed to perform a welfare check on 31-year-old Gareth Williams. Gareth failed to turn up at work last week, and no one had seen or heard from him for about eight days, which was unlike him.

His family was rightfully concerned, as were his colleagues.

There was a moment's pause before the tinny voice on the radio warned Gallagher that he needed to be aware of who Gareth was, or rather, who he worked for. MI6.

When buzzing Gareth's Pimlico apartment, Gallagher didn't garner any response, and in the end, he called the letting agency that held the keys to the building. Gallagher was surprised to find the flat stifling hot when let in, which was strange considering it was the middle of summer.

The curtains are drawn, the place baking like an over. Gallagher is drawn to the woman's bright orange wig hanging off the back of one of the chairs. The wig had little consequence and could have been used for a fancy dress party. Or maybe Gareth just liked it. It seemed incongruous.

The flat is spread across two levels but was exceptionally tidy and spotless upon inspection. Once the first level was checked, Gallagher made his way upstairs, first entering the bedroom. He spotted a crumbled bathrobe on the floor near the door to the ensuite as if someone had thrown it off before going in. The first sign of carelessness in the whole flat.

Stepping over it, the first thing he sees in the ensuite is a red bag in the bath. A North Face branded holder. Gallagher treads to it to get a closer look. The bag was tightly packed, the zips pulled close together with a padlock, and the keys inside the bag.

PC Gallagher's curiosity grew, and he picked up the bag to get a feel. There was quite a weight to it, so much so that he only managed to lift it a few inches. Disturbingly, a drop of red liquid dropped from the bottom onto the porcelain bath. And Gallagher's nostrils are assaulted by the unmistakable stench of decomposing flesh.

Gingerly, Gallagher placed the bag back down and radioed in for assistance.

Detective Sergeant Paul Cogan is soon on the scene, and he cuts open the holdall, revealing a naked adult male in an advanced state of decay.

The body was so contorted that at first, Cogan thinks the arms and legs had been cut off, but the arms were tightly tucked in, and the legs pulled up into a foetal position. The body was soon confirmed to be that of the missing Gareth Williams.

Who was Gareth Wyn Williams? Gareth Williams was described by a fellow cyclist as 'a shy chap' with a 'peculiarly memorable laugh and smile.'[1]

Born on 26 September 1978, Gareth was a Welsh lad who began studying mathematics part-time at Bangor University whilst still in secondary school. He graduated with a first-class degree at seventeen years old. Gareth was exceptionally bright and ambitious to match. His maths teacher at Bodedern Secondary School, Geraint Williams, has praised Gareth as an 'exceptional' pupil who was the 'best logician' he had met. 'If you explained something once to Gareth, he remembered it. You didn't have to explain it again.'[2]

After gaining a PhD at the University of Manchester, he dropped out from a subsequent post-graduate course at St Catherine's College, Cambridge. Instead, he took employment with GCHQ in Cheltenham in 2001, renting a room in Prestbury for nearly a decade. Gloucestershire. GCHQ is the UK's intelligence, security and cyber agency, but it was on a three-year secondment to MI6.[3]

Gareth was known to his friends, colleagues and family as remarkably gifted and hard-working, whose spare time was dedicated to outdoor pursuits: rock climbing, fell running and cycling. He also loved art, fashion, good food and shopping. But he did not get close to many people.

His former landlady in Cheltenham, Jennifer Elliot, depicted him as a 'private person' who 'kept himself to himself'. He was pretty introverted.[4]

There are consequences to being extraordinary, such as loneliness. It couldn't have been easy, always being known as the clever kid and younger than his university peers. But in 2001, his intelligence caught the attention of the British Security Services when he was recruited by GCHQ. Perhaps he has finally found his tribe. The work suited him; it involved intercepting and analysing electronic communications worldwide and allowed him to showcase his advanced math skills.

Given his skill set, it is likely that Gareth's work focused on cryptography and cryptanalysis, meaning he was both a code breaker and maker, able to work in cyber protection and infiltration.

Gareth's death was timed on 16 August 2010. Looking back at the crime scene, identifying the body was the easy part of this case, but the mystery of how he came to be in the bag is not something that can be quickly resolved. There was no sign of struggle in the flat; if there was, it was hidden very well. The shower curtain had been drawn, and the lights were off. A doorknob had been removed, and one of Gareth's four phones had been reset to factory settings. So that could either mean Gareth got into the bag willingly, or he was drugged or already dead when he was put in there.

One prominent element was that someone else must have closed and padlocked the bag. The officers could not see evidence of a break-in or robbery, so if someone else was involved, Gareth likely let them in, which implied that he knew them or did not expect any harm. On the other hand, given Gareth's occupation, the possibility that something as horrific and obscure as this may have been a professional hit cannot be ruled out.

Just as Gallagher and Cogan were mulling it over, the flat was invaded by a unit of unfamiliar, grim-faced officers. Their body language was intense, almost hostile. They told PC Gallagher, 'We will take it from here.' Gallagher and Cogan's part in the investigation was over, and they were hung out to dry.

We don't know who these agents are, where they came from, and why they dismissed Gallagher and Cogan. Are they there to find evidence? Are they there to plant it, or are they there to remove something vital to the investigation?

We know that detectives from Scotland Yard's homicide and serious crime command are forced to wait until the agents have completed their sweep before they are allowed in. This is catastrophic to the investigation itself. When the detectives were allowed in, the place was cleaner than in the first place.

The front door has also been removed and taken away. In fact, in this sweep, Gareth's family allege that crucial DNA evidence was interfered with, and fingerprints left at the scene were wiped off as part of a coverup.[5]

Unsurprisingly, tensions emerged between security services and the police because, as Scotland Yard see it, they have a duty to investigate the sudden death and potential murder of Gareth Willians, but National Security are making it exceptionally difficult.

This is where Jacqueline Sebire comes in. A formidable detective, Sebire spent most of her career moving swiftly up the ranks of Scotland Yard, a part of the new generation of female police officers. She knew she needed to utilise her skill set to resolve this case but faced further difficulties. The terms of the investigation set by protocol: Sebire's team were not allowed direct access to anyone at MI6.

Soon after the investigation began, the head of the Secret Intelligence Service and Metropolitan Police met to discuss how the investigation would be handled, considering the secretive nature of Gareth's work and who would lead the investigation. And there was no end to the hurdles in Sebire's way.

Gareth had recently qualified for operational deployment and had worked with U.S National Security Agency and FBI agents. The U.S. State Department asked that William's work be absent at the inquest. The foreign secretary, William Hague, signed a public interest immunity certificate authorising the withholding of details about Gareth's work and U.S. joint operations from the inquest.[6]

Sebire and her team were not allowed direct access to anyone at MI6, not allowed to know what Gareth was working on, nor given access to any of his colleagues. They cannot ask them questions or make any statements. In other words, they are prevented from examining a vast number of witnesses like any detective would endeavour to in an investigation. Critically, they cannot look these witnesses in the eye, examine their body language and make the call on whether they are telling the truth.

Instead, they must submit questions to another part of the Metropolitan Police, called SO15, whose officers have a higher security clearance. SO15 officers then take those questions to MI6, where they sit with the concerned individuals in their line managers' presence.

What makes this situation worse is that none of the S015 officers make a verbatim record of the answers, which essentially means word for word. Instead, they write up their notes, essentially their version of the truth, and then pass these anonymised notes back to Sebire's team in their role as information conduits.

This is a very elaborate version of Chinese whispers. Things are going to be misconstrued and misinterpreted down the pipeline of communication. Also, imagine having the manager, who dictates your paychecks, present when you are being interviewed by the police; it is not the best way to encourage full disclosure.

They have the power to control what is passed on. Vital details and nuances may be lost.

Naturally, DCI Sebire would prefer primary access to the witnesses, but she accepts that this is the way it must be done publicly, and she trusts the officers. With one line of enquiry blocked, Sebire turns to the public for information. She appeals to the public for anyone who might have seen or had contact with Gareth Williams between the 11th and 23rd of August. She asks if they can come forward to trigger people's memories. Detective released images taken from CCTV footage showing Gareth in the days before his death.

One date-stamped frame dictates his steps on Sunday, 15 August.

In a red t-shirt, beige chinos and white trainers, Gareth's wiry figure is shown shopping in Knightsbridge. Detectives can track his movements from that day through his card transactions.

He drew cash from a cash machine outside Harrods before venturing into the department store to purchase cakes from the food hall. He also picked up a couple of peppered steaks.

That Sunday, you can almost see Gareth's post-annual leave glow; the weather is hot and humid in the images, and he's relaxed. He has recently returned from a trip and is due in the office the next morning, but when CCTV showed Gareth heading towards the block of flats at number 36, he is never seen again. Gareth returns home to his flat. What happens after he closes the door remains a mystery.

What happened in the following nineteen hours holds the key to his death, but there is little to nothing known about those missing hours. Evidence heard at the inquest suggests that during the evening, Gareth cooked one of the peppered grill steaks he had bought from Waitrose that day and had it for his dinner.

There are also indications that at 11.30 pm that evening, he backed up data to a laptop from one of his phones before viewing a cycling website at around 1.00 am in the morning. However, these details cannot be confirmed as it could have been possible that someone else may have been using his phone and computer.

Like the rest of the case, speculation fills the void of those missing hours.

A couple, a man and woman in their thirties, were seen entering the communal area of Gareth's block one evening in June or July. None of his neighbours remember buzzing them or knew who they were, so the assumption is that they had come to see Gareth. E-fits of the couple are released.

Meanwhile, an autopsy of Gareth's body is unable to establish any apparent cause of death. Toxicology examinations are inconclusive, revealing no trace of alcohol or drugs in Gareth's system. So, it wasn't an overdose, and he wasn't poisoned, as far as we know. One issue pathologists have is the length of time between Gareth's death, which we already know occurred in the early hours of Monday, 16 August and his body being found on 23 August. During that time, the heat was on full blast, which accelerated decomposition, making it harder for any meaningful tests to be carried out.

Dr Benjamin Smith, who performed the autopsy, only found minor injuries on Gareth, which could have been a result of accidents. He noted that poison or asphyxiation was the most likely cause of death. Toxicologists said some substances, such as cyanide, chloroform and anaesthetic agents, would not have been detectible.

One key question before the inquest was whether Gareth had locked himself in the bag. Expert witness Peter Faulding said he even tried and failed to seal the bag from inside three hundred times. 'I couldn't say it's impossible, but I think even Houdini would have struggled with this one.'[7] Another expert witness, William MacKay, said that he and an assistant had failed more than one hundred attempts to lock the bag from inside but could not rule out that Gareth had been able to.[8]

Did Gareth die in the bag? Pathologist Dr Richard Shepard thinks, ' The balance of probability is that Gareth was alive when he got in that bag.' He added, 'I think there could have been a period of awareness that he needed to get out. The length of time must have been short.' But Faulding said he believed that Gareth was dead or unconscious before being placed in the bag. He suggested it would have been possible to shut Gareth in the holdall if rigour mortis had not set in.[9]

DCI Sebire had many questions but very few answers, so she needed to start filling in some gaps, so she turned to Gareth's family. Gareth lived in the seaside village of Valley on the island of Anglesey in Wales. With a population of 2361, it is a very tight-knit community. It's a place where everyone knows everyone. Now imagine going from that sort of familial community into the big impersonal city of London. Where no matter how physically close your neighbours are, you might never find out their names. It must have been a challenging adjustment for Gareth to forsake everything and everyone you knew for your career. He may have felt very isolated in London, especially given the secretive nature of his work. Who could he confide in?

When Gareth's body was discovered, his parents were out of the country, so the first to hear the news was Grandpa John, who was so shocked that he fell and had to be taken to hospital.

Gareth's sister, Ceri, told the detectives that she last saw her brother alive in June when Gareth took her and her husband to tea at The Ritz to celebrate their second wedding anniversary. Gareth was buoyant. The three of them spent the afternoon laughing and chatting. Since then, Ceri has regularly contacted her brother over the phone. She hadn't noticed anything unusual, and the last time she could get through to him was 11 August.

Ceri revealed more personal information about Gareth that only a sister would know: that Gareth was on secondment to MI6. It was meant to be a three-year term, but Gareth was unhappy. He disliked the macho office culture. It sounds like there was some friction, and he wanted to cut his time short at MI6 and move back to Cheltenham at the beginning of September. Was this cutting of ties disagreed upon by MI6 to almost drastic measures?

This was a question Ceri could not answer. She can only tell the police about the Gareth she knew, a generous, loving brother. They had the kind of relationship where they told each other everything. Sebire hoped this would be advantageous because she wanted more insight into Gareth's personal life, particularly if he had a girlfriend.

No, as far as his sister knew, but that does not explain the £20,000 worth of women's clothing that police found in Gareth's flat. And these were expensive designer brands such as Stella McCartney and Louboutin. There were clothes, shoes, wigs and even make-up, most of it still in its original packaging. We all know that clothing should not have a gender; clothes do not care who wears them, but police recovered receipts that show Gareth had been buying clothes for over two years. At just five feet and eight inches and with a slim figure, it's possible that Gareth could have fit into the clothes at a pinch, but they would have fit his sister, Ceri, more comfortably. If Gareth wanted to wear the clothes, why didn't he get them to accommodate his size?

Ceri believes that the clothes were brought for her or one of Gareth's close friends, Sian Lloyd-Jones, a fashion stylist he had known since childhood. Sian confirmed that Gareth had bought her a Gucci bag, a Mulberry bag and Armani fur, and he did the same for his sister. Ceri and Sian believed they were bound to receive the clothing, as it was just how generous Gareth was.

However, this did not stop rumours circulating in December 2010. Several newspapers reported that shortly before his death, Gareth went to a performance by drag artist Johnny Wu at The Bistro Tech club in East London. I do not see anything unusual about this because drag is an art everyone should appreciate.

It is also claimed that his internet browsing history indicated that he had visited a bondage-related website.

There was also a possible sighting of Gareth at a gay bar in the Vauxhall area. It was also reported that cocaine, gay pornography and S&M paraphernalia were found in Gareth's flat and that he frequently paid for male escorts. None of this is true. In fact, Gareth didn't really drink in excess.[10]

Gareth's friends and family thought these rumours were a false narrative spun by security services to deflect suspicion from themselves and to smear Gareth's name. Naturally, Sebire condemned the reporting of outright lies. However, she defends the release of some details because they may prompt someone to come forward, probably because she hit a brick wall with MI6. There was one theory she wanted to focus on.

She focused on the theory that Gareth's death had nothing to do with his work but related to his personal life. One of the elements of his personal life was BDSM.

Although Ceri would say that Gareth was the 'most scrupulous risk assessor' she had ever known, he had interests that his sister – to whom he was arguably closer than anyone else – did not know about, which may have caused considerable risks if not done correctly. Bondage.[11]

It may have been no more than curiosity that drew Gareth to view the bondage website, but he may have taken his interests to another level. In 2007, Gareth's landlady, Jennifer Elliot, was woken in the middle of the night by Gareth's cries for help. She and her husband found him in his boxer shorts, lying on his bed, his hands tied to the knobs of the headboard.

In a statement, Jennifer was told by Gareth that he just wanted to see if he could free himself. Jennifer and her husband thought the escapade was a sexual act rather than an attempt at escapology, and Gareth promised his landlady that he would not attempt it again.

However, Gareth was in London for two years, which would have afforded him ample opportunities to experiment. The investigation did not reveal that Gareth had shared such interests with anyone, let alone invited them back to his flat to partake in them. But secrecy is the MI6 officers' trade, so if he wanted to keep something private, he would figure out a way.

Given the sensitivity of his work, would this side of Gareth have any relevance to his death? If Gareth was gay or had an interest in women's clothing or bondage, it may be that he wanted to keep this aspect of his life hidden. He may have been scared of the blackmail or bullying in the workplace due to his views on the culture. However, from an MI6 point of view, none of this would have been an issue.

Speaking anonymously about the security vetting process, one agent explains that there is no template for what the individual should be or what their lifestyle should be. Individuals have their lifestyles and sexuality that are perfectly legitimate. In other words, owning women's clothing and being gay would not have presented a security risk.

So, what do we know so far?

We know that Gareth had a very secretive job, and we know he may have felt isolated due to the difference in culture between Wales and London. He liked to buy women's clothing, may have been gay and may have experimented in bondage. But we still do not know why his body was found in a North Face Holdall in his bathtub.

Another clue in Gareth's flat was provided by a newspaper clipping under a book on his living room table. From an Observer article, the cutting listed the 'top five regrets of the dying', among them having the courage to 'live a life true to myself,' 'express my feelings' and 'let myself be happier.' This suggests that those unexplained hours of Gareth William's life were probably unhappy. But it still doesn't explain what happened.

DCI Sebire and her team kept an open mind as they reviewed the main theories in this case. The first set is dependent on Gareth being alone when he dies.

Theory one: suicide. He got into the bag, knowing he would die from asphyxiation. However, there are more accessible and more obvious ways of killing yourself.

Theory two: his death was accidental while performing an erotic act involving bondage and self-asphyxiation. However, as Ceri described him, Gareth was a scrupulous risk assessor, so would he have gone into the bag without some means of escape or a backup plan?

Theory three: Gareth was training himself in escapology. This may seem far-fetched, but when is true crime ever simple. Nevertheless, Gareth had recently been cleared for active deployment in the field. He may have been acting out scenarios requiring him to find his way out of a tight spot. There was a padlock inside the bag with him.

The next set of theories is reliant on there being a third party.

Theory four: Gareth was murdered by a professional hitman sent by a foreign power or a criminal gang whose activities Gareth was investigating. Remember how the central heating was up in the middle of August, and it sped up decomposition? It may not have been a coincidence.

Theory five: he was murdered by someone within MI6. As shocking as this may seem, at the inquest into Gareth's death in 2021, the coroner described it as a legitimate line of inquiry. It probably doesn't help that it took a week for anyone at MI6 to explore Gareth's unexplained absence, something they did apologise for.

The coroner surmised that most of the fundamental questions concerning how Gareth died remained unanswered. Still, she was adamant that a third party moved the bag containing Gareth into the bath. 'The cause of his death was unnatural and likely to have been criminally mediated,' she added. 'I am therefore satisfied that on the balance of probabilities, Gareth was killed unlawfully.'[12]

Theory six: he died accidentally as a result of a BDSM encounter that went wrong. Despite there being no evidence of Gareth having sexual partners, it is a possibility. Some of these theories seem implausible, but as one detective says, 'If you can imagine it, then we are investigating it.'

Within Occam's Razor process of elimination, we need to think about how the theories fit into the evidence. If Gareth was alone when he got into the bag, he could have only done so when it was already in the bath, so you would expect to find his fingerprints and DNA on the rim as he lowered himself in. But there were no traces of either, suggesting that someone else had placed the bag in the bath with Gareth already inside it.

Intriguingly, police found no trace of Gareth's prints or DNA on the bag's padlock or zipper, but they do find fragments of unidentified DNA there, which they believe are from two individuals. They also find traces of Gareth's blood on the outside of the bag.

Intriguingly, police found no trace of Gareth's prints or DNA on the bag's padlock or zipper, but they do find fragments of unidentified DNA there, which they believe are from two individuals. They also find traces of Gareth's blood on the outside of the bag.

Police also discover the presence of unidentified DNA components on the green towel found in Gareth's kitchen. More significantly, a two-millimetre piece of hair found on Gareth's hand contains unidentified DNA. This could be the most concrete proof that someone else was involved in the orchestration of Gareth's death.

DCI Sebire and her team ruled out the first bundle of theories as she was convinced that someone else was involved in his death. Could it be the mysterious couple who police believed visited Gareth beforehand? But by March 2012, eighteen months after Gareth's death, they were still not found.

Gareth's family believe that MI6 are to blame for this. The agency had some difficult questions to answer, such as why they took so long to check up on Gareth when he failed to turn up for work. The family's suspicions ran even deeper when solicitor Anthony O'Toole argued that the family's impression was that the unknown third party was a member of some agency specialising in the dark arts of the Secret Service or some vital evidence had been removed. Let's not forget there was a short time when some agents entered the crime scene first and even took the front door.

It would also have been physically impossible for Gareth to wipe the bathroom clean after he got into the bag.

Furthermore, DCI Sebire only learned about nine memory sticks found at MI6 during the inquest, and the coroner questioned the impartiality of a vetted police officer who liaised with MI6. This is vital information that the officers of SO15 should have made them aware of as soon as possible. Questions were also asked about whether electronic material had been secured adequately at MI6 to prevent interference.

Those details, which could be explained by sloppiness, do little to dispel the view held in some quarters that MI6 was not fully transparent and, in turn, the theory that they were somehow involved in the death or cleaned up.

Dr Wilcox says most of the fundamental questions about how Gareth died remain unanswered. She agrees with pathologists that the most likely cause of death was carbon dioxide suffocation, which would have occurred within three minutes of Gareth getting inside the holdall, or an undetected fast-acting poison may have been involved that toxicologists could not have picked up.

She concluded that the cause of his death was unnatural and likely to have been criminally mediated.

An investigation into the handling of the case goes underway, focusing on the unacceptable communication breakdown between Scotland Yard and MI6, to the point where significant change to the process was made. Homicide detectives will be able to go to MI6 personnel directly without having to go through an SO15.

If we look at the coroner's view that Gareth was killed via a third party because there is no way he could have closed the padlock himself on the bag after the inquest, a retired sergeant in the Royal Artillery blew up this theory. Jim Fetherstonhaugh approached the police, claiming to have pulled off that feat. He showed that it was possible to zip up the bag from the inside and clock the padlock closed by manipulating it through the bag's fabric with his fingers.[13]

All that remains is to push out with his body so that the two zippers are squeezed together. There is no proof that this is what Gareth did, but it shows that something previously thought impossible is possible.

November 2013, Detective Assistant Commissioner Martin Hewitt calls a press briefing at New Scotland Yard, ready to announce the findings of a major three–year investigation into Gareth William's death.

Hewitt tells the reporters that despite the considerable effort, there is insufficient evidence to be definitive on the circumstances that led to Gareth's death. But Detective Assistant Commissioner Martin Hewitt said the police could not 'fundamentally and beyond doubt' rule out the possibility that a third party was involved in his death. For that reason, he concludes that Gareth most likely died alone.

'Rather, what we are left with is either individual pieces of evidence, or a lack of such evidence, that can logically support one of a number of hypotheses.'[14]

This is a devastating blow to Gareth's family, and they are convinced that the police have got it wrong and the original verdict remains correct. The police may have closed the case, but that does not mean it is the end.

There are never-ending theories about what happened to Gareth, including the idea that Gareth was killed because he was close to identifying a Russian mole in the UK security services.

Several DNA traces were recovered from Gareth's flat. Analysis at the time proved inconclusive, but recent advances in DNA sciences mean that today's experts may get the necessary vital results. No other future developments were made in the case, and in the sense of Occam's Razor, there is not even enough substantial evidence to boil down to a substantial theory. However, I do not think the most probable theory is that he locked himself in a bag unless he worked for the Cirque du Soleil. We can firmly say Occam's Razor did not work in this situation or didn't even get the chance to work because of the lack of evidence.

If we use Occam's Razor, we could suppose that as a mathematician, Gareth liked puzzles, and a conundrum such as locking himself in a bag and getting himself out again may have given him an exciting challenge; however, as we have already specified, he would have made sure he had an escape plan.

However, is it more likely that Gareth's line of work got him into some sticky situations where he had to be killed to be removed? Potentially, you would think secret services would have better ways to hide a body. However, maybe that is the beauty of this whole situation. The way they left his body was so peculiar and bewildering; they had the benefit of the doubt because the finger could not be pointed at them fully.

It can be said that the case of Gareth William is a poignant example that simplicity is a limitation in true crime and cannot always be relied on as an answer. Nevertheless, it is bittersweet that Gareth's case cannot be fully put to rest, and his family cannot be granted the closure they deserve.

Chapter Nine

What Happened to Mike Williams?

Tallahassee is home to approximately forty-eight lakes, offering residents and visitors the chance to boat, canoe and hunt fish. Many of the lakes are shallow and highly vegetated, so it is common for residents to travel around sixty miles northwest of Tallahassee to Lake Seminole.

Lake Seminole encompasses 37,500 acres of water and is a great place to fish. But one thing visitors do not know is that it is home to countless alligators. Alligators are known to grow nearly 14 feet long and weigh over 600 pounds.[1]

They can seem scary at first, but that is very misleading. Most of the time, they are very peaceful animals and rarely attack unless provoked. The attacks are relatively rare and have an even slimmer chance of being eaten by one. However, in Lake Seminole, there are so many alligators that authorities recommend visitors steer clear of any areas of marsh or brush.

But alligators were not going to stop Mike Williams from having a good time.

Saturday 16 December 2000 was looking up for Jerry Michael Williams, otherwise known as Mike. Mike and his wife Denise had planned to leave later that afternoon to visit Apalachicola on a romantic getaway to celebrate their 6th wedding anniversary. Before they had to go, Mike thought he would get in some valuable alone time duck hunting at Lake Seminole, which was sixty miles northwest of his home.[2]

The winter hunting season was short-lived, so he wanted to make the most of it. Denise wasn't concerned. Mike was an experienced hunter and dependable. He was going to get home in time for their trip. He was the kind of husband who always put his wife first and would never do anything purposefully to upset Denise. Mike had promised to be home by noon, but he wasn't.

Instantly concerned, Denise didn't wait to see if he was running late; she immediately spread the word that Mike was missing. Denise trusted her husband but was well aware of the dangers of Lake Seminole. Accidents happened, and the lake was infested with alligators. I don't think Occam has to state the obvious here.

Jerry Michael Williams loved two things above all else: his family and spending time outdoors. The 31-year-old worked long hours as a real estate appraiser to provide for his wife and their eighteen-month-old daughter. His six-figure salary afforded them a comfortable lifestyle in Tallahassee, but Mike worked hard for his money. It was a by-product of being raised by upstanding and selfless working-class parents, who sacrificed a lot to give Mike and his brother a quality upbringing.

His mother, Cheryl, worked as a daycare worker, and his father, Jerry Senior, worked as a Greyhound bus driver. The Williams family were not wealthy, but they were comfortable and chose to raise Mike and his brother in a trailer to save for their education.

They were able to send Mike and his older brother Nick to a private school, North Florida Christian School. Mike was a popular boy, often described as the kind of person who would do anything and everything for you. Although Mike was the type of man who would hang out with anyone, he spent most of his time with Brian Winchester, a fellow freshman he met on their first day of high school, and they were inseparable ever since.

In the American school movie fashion, Mike starts dating an unflappable, stoic Christian girl called Denise Merrill, and they are the power couple dominating the yearbook. Mike and Denise often went on double dates with Brian and his girlfriend Kathy, a fellow North Florida Christian School cheerleader. The four students were so close that they all attended Florida State University together after high school graduation. Denise majored in Accounting, while Mike majored in City Planning and Political science.[3]

Ever the hard worker, Mike started working at Ketcham Realty and Appraisal Group. Upon graduating in 1991, he accepted a full-time position as a real estate appraiser while Denise worked as an accountant. In 1994, Mike and Denise tied the knot with Brian as his best man.

In 1999, Brian and Katy Winchester welcomed a son, and the next year, Mike and Denise followed suit and welcomed their daughter, Ainsley.

Mike worked hard for his money, leaving him very little leisure time, so whenever he did fit in some time for himself, he headed to one of the nearby lakes to go duck hunting. Mike had taken up this sport during his teens, allowing him to enjoy fresh air and peace in the surrounding woods.

Mike loaded his gear into his Green Ford Bronco, attaching his small motorised boat to the tow bar, and drove into the pre-dawn light.

One of the first people Denise contacted about Mike's disappearance was her father, Warren Merril.

Warren contacted the Florida Fish and Wildlife Conservation Commission, also known as the FWC. The organisation was the first point of contact for managing public waters and initiating search and rescue missions. They also worked closely with various law enforcement to investigate any critical incidents.

Within ten minutes of Warren's calls, officers from the FWC arrived at Lake Seminole. There are over 37 ½ thousand acres to explore, and an overwhelming feeling is palpable. *Where on earth would you start to look for Mike?* A helicopter was ready to sweep over the area, but the cold snap in the weather forced the aircraft to wait until the conditions improved.

Meanwhile, FWC officers set out into the wilderness on foot but failed to uncover Mike, his boat, or his car. At this point, deputies from the Jackson County Sheriff's Department were also brought in to assist, focusing on areas Mike was known to hunt in the past. Word spread like wildfire amongst Mike's friends and family, and they did not fail to head to the lake to aid in the search. Denise was beside herself, emotionally distressed and sobbing, but *she never went to the lake.*

The hours trickled away without any breakthroughs, and it was beginning to look bleak for Mike. At 9.00 pm, the helicopter was finally cleared to fly, but it was grounded by midnight as they had found nothing of significance. This did not deter the ground search party, and as the stormy winter night made its appearance, they embraced it as they continued to track the swampy, foggy terrain. The only source of warmth was a drum fire that served as the unofficial search quarters.

When Brian received word that Mike was missing, he did not hesitate to join in the search and at 2.30 am, he and his father, Marcus, ventured around the western side of Lake Seminole. They reached an area colloquially known as Stump Field in honour of the many dead tree stumps that jutted from the waters. They shone their flashlights through the reeds and trees while calling out Mike's name. Then, Marcus spotted something in the water approximately seventy meters south of a boat ramp. Mike's boat.

An FWC officer was notified and quickly secured the vessel containing Mike's hunting equipment, including his duck decoys, lifejacket and shotgun. There was no sign of Mike and nothing untoward about the boat itself. His shotgun was still in its case, and there was no mud in the ship, so it didn't look like Mike had been mid-hunt when something occurred, and he had to leave.

Mike's Ford Bronco was found roughly seventy meters away, and there was no indication of Mike's whereabouts. The only possible clue lay in the boat: although the motor was dead, the engine was switched to the 'On' position, so it should have been in use when it was abandoned.

Stump Field was filled with roots, weeds and tree stumps, some of which weren't distinguishable from the surface. So officers speculated that Mike could have been on his boat, hit a submerged stump, and the impact threw him overboard. When he left home, the boots he had been wearing were inside the boat, meaning he was likely wearing waders when he went missing. Made from waterproof fabric, such as PVC rubber, waders consist of boots permanently attached to a pair of overalls. Favoured by fishermen and duck hunters, the wearer can stand in water without getting wet.

On the other hand, if someone were to fall into the water while wearing them, the weight of the water could pull them down, while the pressure of the water could also cause the fabric to suction onto their skin. Removing them and dragging the wearer down to murky depths is difficult.

Although the lake was only eight feet deep maximum, if Mike's waders filled with water, he could have been dragged under the surface, which is what the officers hypothesized. His boat could have continued without him until it stopped, potentially hitting a muddy bank.

One officer thought that when they found the waders, Mike couldn't be far behind.

At first light on Sunday, 17 December, FWC officers entered the water in a boat designed to navigate Stump Field's heavily vegetated waters. A thorough grid search was conducted across the lake, with officers tying ropes from one tree stump to another to mark each area that had been examined. They used poles to poke around the murky waters every six to eight inches to differentiate the feel of a human body from any other underwater debris. Underwater cameras capable of monitoring movement were also mounted along the gridlines in case anything was missed. Divers coursed the waterway, and cadaver dogs were recruited whilst helicopters and field wing aeroplanes continued the search from above.

In other words, no stone was left unturned.

Mike's friends, family and other volunteers braved the cold weather to aid the search, which continued for the next week. People were cautiously optimistic that Mike could have made it to a nearby island and was waiting to be rescued, but it wasn't very likely. It was beginning to look more likely that Mike had drowned. FWC officers had learnt from other incidents that it could sometimes take up to seven days for a body to rise to the surface, especially in freezing temperatures. But it had been over a week, so something should have turned up by then.

There had been around eighty known deaths caused by drowning in that very lake, and every single body had been recovered, so this made no sense. By Christmas Day, any hopes of finding Mike alive had vanished, and it just became a search for his body. The search was scaled back to just one FWC officer patrolling the waters and one flight a day checking overhead.

The subsequent discovery was on 27 December. The FWC officer noticed a bit of fabric floating in the shallow water amongst some grass and trees. It was a distinctive camouflage hunting hat, shown to Denise, who confirmed it looked like one owned by Mike. Brian was at the lake when Mike's hat was found and even had a photo of them, with Mike wearing it, to identify it. An exhaustive search was conducted of the shallow waters where the hat was found, with the expectation that Mike's body would be lingering under the surface, but nothing.

Mike's mother. Cheryl took matters into her own hands and hired a private search and rescue team to comb the area, but they also failed to find any sign of Mike. Consequentially inciting fuel to another theory that had been getting traction. That Mike had been eaten by alligators.

Up to twenty alligators had been spotted in the area on the first night of the search alone. Maybe one of them had gotten to Mike's body before it had a chance to be found.

Denise, potentially for the sake of closure, accepted the alligator theory and scheduled a memorial service, which was held on 11 February 2001, the day after the search for Mike was officially called off.

By this point, Mike had been missing for forty-four days, and an area of over five acres had been thoroughly inspected. A report written by the Florida Boating Accident Investigation Report on 23 February 2001, was starkly inconclusive: 'Nothing in investigative or search and rescue efforts has produced any definitive evidence of a boating accident or a fatality as of this date. Mr Williams is still missing.'

By February, Denise struggled to make ends meet; she no longer had Mike's salary to help, and she was raising a toddler alone. Denise would not get any sort of insurance payout without a body or proof that Mike was actually dead. So, in the hope of getting some financial relief, Denise requested that Mike be declared dead. A court hearing was scheduled for the end of June 2001.

Could there be a rational explanation for this behaviour? Understandably, Denise was having to get used to being a single parent with only one source of income and must have wanted closure, but was she even hoping Mike would turn up alive?

On 22 June, around a week before the court hearing, a fisherman was out on Lake Seminole near Stump Field when he found Mike's waders floating near the water's surface. Still hanging around the waist of the waders was Mike's pouch, filled with shotgun shells. It was a surprising find, considering drivers had spent fifty-six days combing through each inch of the area. And the evidence turns up just before a court case declaring Mike dead? Divine intervention at its finest.

The waders were found partially inside out as if Mike had taken them off. There were no bite marks or other tears, meaning they couldn't have

1. William of Ockham, from a stained glass window at a church in Surrey.

2. Illustration of William of Ockham, from a 1341 manuscript of Ockham's Summa Logicae.

3. Photo of Jane Britton.

4. Example of Red Ochre.

5. Craigie Arms, 6 Bennett Street, Cambridge, Massachusetts, USA. This building is on the National Register of Historic Places.

6. Photo of Jacob Wetterling.

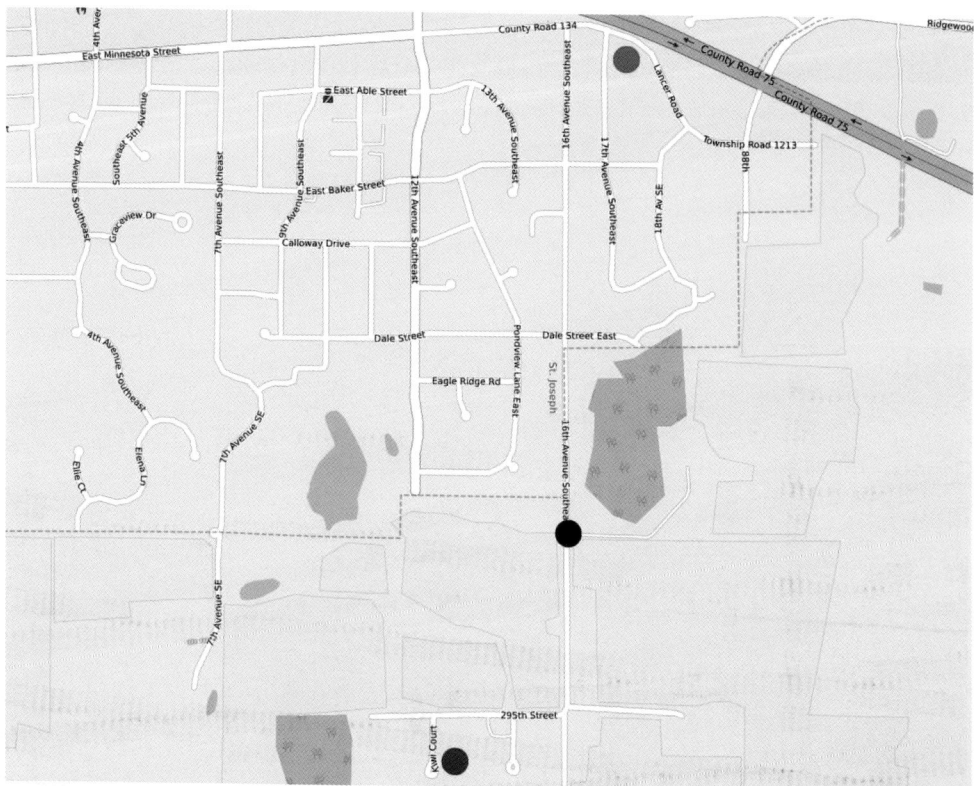

7. This map highlights key locations related to the Jacob Wetterling case. The circles represent the former Tom Thumb convenience store, the site of the kidnapping, and Jacob Wetterling's home.

8. Jacob's Final Resting Place.

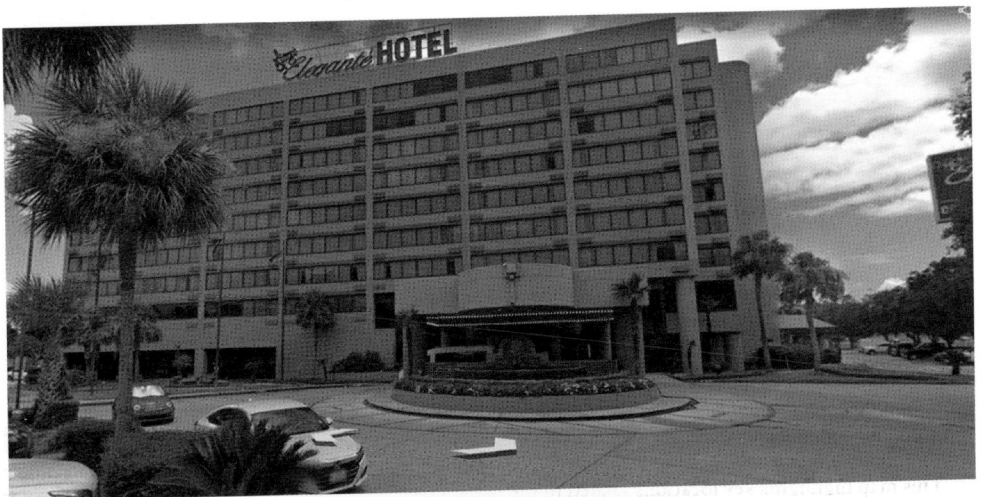

9. The MCM Elegante Hotel where Greg Fleniken had his fateful stay.

10. One of the first monuments on Jerika Bink's run; the Mount Timpanogos Utah Temple, American Fork, Utah.

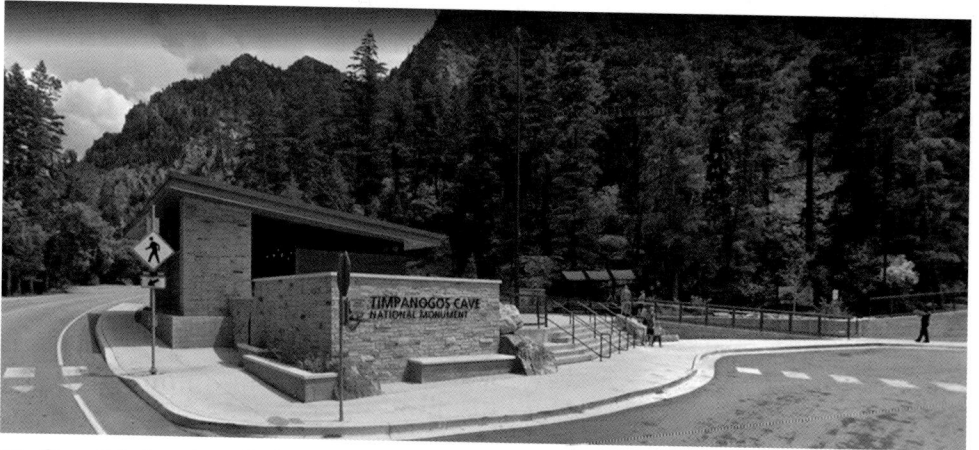

11. One of the last places Jerika Binks's was seen; the Timpanogos Cave National Monument.

12. The grave of Gareth Wyn Williams, Translated from Welsh, the inscription on the headstone reads: In loving memory of Gareth Wyn Williams. Mathematician. Son and a special brother. 1978–2010.

13. Joseph and Summer McStay with their 4- and 3-year sons, Gianni and Joseph Jr.

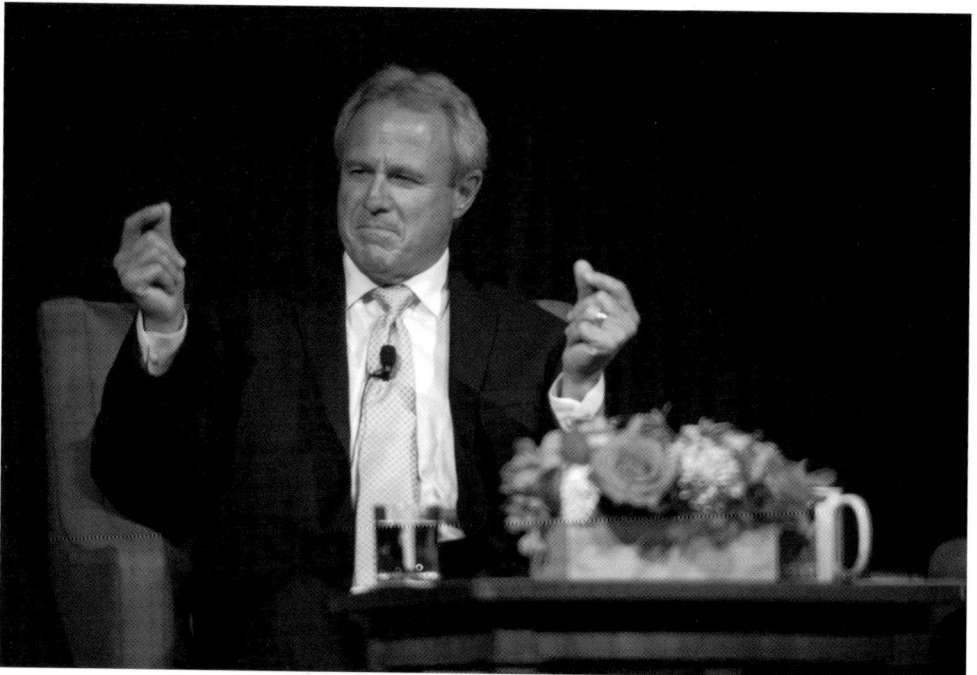

14. Michael Morton, author of 'Getting Life.' Morton was exonerated on October 4, 2011 after spending nearly 25 years in a Williamson County prison after being wrongly convicted of the murder of his wife.

been taken off Mike by an alligator or predator. No DNA evidence was found linking the clothing to Mike, regardless. Nevertheless, a week later, a Leon County judge granted Denise William's petition to have Mike declared legally dead based on those recovered items and an assumption that alligators and other water life had consumed the body in its entirety.

This was a rare move in a case without a body, as in Florida, it typically took five years for a person to be declared dead when there was no proof. Mike's mother was infuriated with the ruling because some aspects of the case still did not add up.

What would have happened if Mike's disappearance had been treated as foul play rather than as a result of natural causes?

First, Mike's boat was found with its engine off and in the on position with the gas tank full. Would the engine be off if Mike had fallen off and drowned? If the boat manufacturers had been contacted during the initial investigation, they would have discovered that if there was no one to guide the motor, the boat would have run around in circles until the gas ran out. After that, according to weather reports, the empty boat would have been blown into the westerly direction by the storm that rolled in that day, meaning his boat would have come to a rest across the lake on the opposite shore, not 225ft from his vehicle. What doesn't help is that the boat was released to the family without being searched for DNA, fingerprints or other evidence.

If authorities had interviewed Mike's friends and family, they would have heard that he was a very safe and careful hunter; he never went hunting alone and always had someone with him. Suddenly, the idea that he went hunting alone in the morning before his anniversary trip did not seem feasible.

He also never wore waders on the boat. He would wait to put them on. Mike was obsessed with safety, so much so that he would lecture his friends about it because he knew if he fell into the lake and his waders filled with water, he would drown.

The theory of Mike's waders filling with water is starting to lose credibility. As was the theory that he was eaten by alligators. At the beginning of this chapter, we had already established that alligators are territorial, but attacks are sporadic. The FDLE spoke with alligator specialists who said that alligators had unlikely eaten Mike. Firstly, it was winter, and North Florida alligators slowed down and became sluggish in cold weather. It's akin to a form of hibernation but for cold-blooded animals. If, by some irrational chance, an alligator did eat Mike, it was impossible that no evidence was left behind, and nothing was found.

We can see where we are heading now if Mike's death was not accidental. Maybe he disappeared intentionally for his own reasons. But how likely was this? Mike loved his wife and daughter; would he leave them behind for no reason? Those close to Mike immediately shut down the idea that he could have staged his own death, he would never abandon his daughter, and he would never abandon his responsibilities. Mike's father had recently passed away, so Mike would never leave his widowed mother or intentionally cause her more pain. Furthermore, Mike and Denise had some exciting plans coming up in the future; they were going to take a cruise to Hawaii and take a business trip to Jamaica. They also wanted to start trying for another baby.

It doesn't seem viable that Mike would run away for no reason, but it always looks like that on the surface. But underneath, people are more complex, and there is always a hidden story that is never read out loud. Maybe he had a secret agenda. This case would never be simple because *people are not simple*.

Cheryl was not prepared to accept that her son was really dead.[4]

He had jokingly mentioned that he would love to get his hands on $50,000 and take a year off. His life insurance, should he fake his death, could have provided that to him. But Cheryl felt in her gut that something was awry and was beginning to think that Mike had been the victim of foul play.

Investigators had not explored this possibility because all they were looking for was a missing hunter, nothing more. Cheryl vowed to uncover the truth and bring Mike home, no matter what. So, she took it upon herself to look further into the case and crosscheck all the details.

Cheryl compiled all of the questionable elements of Mark's disappearance into a twenty-seven-page document. The boat findings, the alligators, and other elements were reported to various law enforcement agencies, urging them to reopen the case. She was relentless in her efforts, but investigators slowly stopped returning her calls as the months and years trickled by. While they felt for Cheryl, there was little they could do.

That didn't deter her; she had connections to the Florida Department of Law Enforcement. After seeking their input in 2004, they finally agreed to open an investigation into Mike's disappearance. After examining all of the peculiar elements of the case, they decided that something did not seem quite right. Investigators changed the status of Mike William's case to a suspicious missing person, which meant it was officially considered criminal. Cheryl was relieved that she was finally being taken seriously.

For years, people regarded Cheryl's relentlessness as a consequence of her grief. Losing your son, realising your grandchild had lost their father, can take its toll on you. But with law enforcement on her side, it proved she was right to question the facts. But this relentlessness did put a strain on Cheryl and Denise's relationship.

When she found out a criminal investigation was going ahead, she was firmly against it. She understood Cheryl's grief, but she wanted to focus on the future rather than dwelling on the past. She had even started dating again. Denise warned Cheryl that if she proceeded with the investigation, Cheryl would no longer have access to her granddaughter. The thought of losing her daughter was devastating, but finding justice for her son was paramount.

We know that Mike had no enemies and was liked by everyone he knew; we also know that there were no witnesses at the lake on that day, and no evidence had been preserved or examined, so investigators had their work cut out for them.

Cheryl did what she could to garner public attention to the case, appealing to journalists, using her retirement savings to have billboards around the town, and publishing ads in a local newspaper appealing directly to readers.

The investigators soldiered on slowly, and the gut feeling felt by all was that Mike did not die in Lake Seminole. By 2007, there was enough technological advancement to warrant a new search of the lake, but it was another dead end, and eventually, cases like this do what they do and go cold.

But Cheryl was still unyielding, and something else nagging at her made her uneasy. *Denise.*

Why was she so quick to accept the drowning explanation and move on? She had kept a low profile throughout the ordeal and had refused to speak to the press, preferring to mourn in private and move on with her life. Her hostility with the case concerned Cheryl; to make matters worse, Denise remarried five years after Mike vanished.

People can mourn however they see fit; they can also move on whenever they see fit, but Denise hasn't just married anyone. She married Mike's best friend, Brian Winchester.

When the couple first went public with their relationship, they were adamant that their romantic interest was a recent development, but people will do what they do, and they will talk. They began speculating that they could have seen each other when Mike was still alive, which was motive enough to want him out of the picture.

Denise had previously returned Mike's hunting equipment to his family, but when Mike's brother went through it in 2007, he noticed that Mike's 22 calibre Ruger pistol was missing. Mike had inherited that gun from his father, so Nick wanted it back. Denise claimed she had lost the gun and even claimed it on insurance. Another red flag.

Nick was persistent like his mother and did not believe a gun could just go missing, so he filed a court order to get it back. Denise eventually returned the firearm to Mike's family, and while they were relieved to have it back, why did she need to lie?

Cheryl's suspicions against Denise were mounting, and they got worse when she realised who would be the sole beneficiary of Mike's insurance policy. Mike had three policies. Valued roughly at $1.75 million, on which Denise was the sole beneficiary. Having declared Mike dead, she was allowed to claim on these within six months of him going missing. She applied to receive the payout just nineteen days after Mike's disappearance.

Law enforcement agreed that these elements were suspicious, and in 2008, cold case investigators re-examined the case with an emphasis on these aspects. Denise's desire to promptly claim Mike's life insurance. After having her baby, Denise quit her job as an accountant to be a stay-at-home mum, and Mike was the sole breadwinner. So, when he went missing, the bills piled up quickly. Denise had been so strapped for cash she even enlisted some of Mike's friends to sell some of his belongings.

But the time at which Mike had taken out the policies did strike the investigators as anomalous; the largest policy, valued at $1 million, was only put in place a few months before his disappearance, and the person who sold him the policy was Brian Winchester.

In Florida, charges relating to insurance fraud carry a five-year statute of limitations. Still, in exceptional circumstances, these can be extended by three years. Mike's case, which was not eight years old, was taken on by state investigators from the Insurance Fraud Division and given immediate priority, and Brian was brought in for questioning.

But Brian denied having anything to do with Mike's disappearance. He told investigators that Mike had already put the feelers out there for taking a higher life insurance policy since becoming a parent, and Brian had simply helped facilitate this.

Furthermore, on 16 December, Brian had an alibi. He said he was happily married to his wife Kathy, and on that morning, he was supposed to join his father-in-law for an early morning hunting trip, but Brian had overslept and had to cancel at the last minute.

Brian's ex-wife, Kathy, verified his alibi, but she said their marriage had been far from happy, and she voiced her suspicions that Brian and Denise could have started an affair well before they went public with their relationship in 2004. If this was the case, it added further weight to the growing theory that Brian and Denise could be behind Mike's disappearance. The problem was that there was nothing to prove the pair had been romantically involved then. Phone and credit card records from the time were no longer available, leaving investigators with no way of linking the two.

They were hitting a brick wall at this point, so the case was closed reluctantly. It could only be opened again if fresh and compelling evidence emerged.

Cheryl was undeterred, she picketed in front of the church that Denise and Brian attended, holding up signs with her son's face on them that read 'Bring Mike Home.' But nothing would happen until 2016.

By 2016, Mike had been missing for almost 16 years.

The morning of Friday, 6 August, started typically for now 46-year-old Denise. At 9.00 am, she got into her Chevrolet Suburban SUV to drive to Florida State University for work; part of Densie's routine was to call her sister. Taking out her phone to dial her sister's number, she glanced in her rear-view mirror only to see a dark figure sitting in her back seat.

It took Denise a moment to realise that the figure was her husband, Brian Winchester. The past four years had not been smooth sailing for the couple; a series of affairs on both parts led Brian to admit that he was a sex addict, and the pair separated in 2012. While Brian had hoped they could work things out, Denise had filed for divorce, citing irreconcilable differences.

Brian grabbed the mobile from Denise's hands and demanded she start driving. She refused but realised that Brian was holding something in his hands. A pistol. He rammed the weapon into Denise's ribs and once again demanded that she start driving. This time, she did as she was told but did not take the route Brian was telling her to. A pharmacy near her home was under constant video surveillance, so Denise drove there instead. Parking as close to the door as possible so she could attract help if need be.

Brian told Denise he was only doing this because she refused to return any calls, emails or messages.

The last few years had been a struggle for Brian. On top of his impending divorce, his mother was suffering from terminal cancer, and he had recently lost custody of his son after the teenager found explicit photos on Brian's phone of Brian engaging with sex workers.

Brian told Denise that if she went ahead with the divorce, he would have nothing to live for and was threatening to end his life. [5]

Denise did anything she could to calm him down. She wouldn't tell anybody about the incident if he let her go. She reassured Brian that he could turn his life around if he tried and invited him to come to her house later so they could talk properly. After forty-five minutes, he seemed to snap out of it and started apologising profusely. His demeanour changed so much that Denise found it hard to believe that this was the same man who violently threatened her just moments ago. Denise took Brian back to his truck, and he went to retrieve some of his belongings from the back of the SUV. Denise took note of the items: a large piece of fabric, a plastic sheet, a spray bottle of bleach and a small hammer-sized tool of some kind. I have never murdered anyone before, but that does sound like a DIY kit and something to be concerned about.

When Brian was out of sight, Denise drove straight to the county.

She was taken straight to an interrogation room, where she provided a complete account of her ordeal, and a warrant was issued immediately for Brian Winchester's arrest. Denise was praised for her actions and quick thinking. Yet, the officers were also aware of her connection to the Mike Williams case, and her kidnapping story raised some eyebrows. They immediately wondered what reason Brian would want Denise dead. Was it possible that she threatened to come clean about what happened to Mike?

Denise was scared that Brian would come after her again, and she immediately requested to file a restraining order against him. Realising how bad their marriage had become, investigators seized this opportunity by the horns. They wanted to turn Denise against Brian just enough so that she would reveal what really happened to Mike.

They grilled her and grilled her, saying that Brian did it and that he held it over her head forever, which is why he made plans to kill her. But she wasn't budging and disputed the theory, mainly focusing on the day's events and getting Brian's restraining order charged. While being interrogated, Brian was arrested and charged with kidnapping, domestic assault and armed burglary.

Brian denied having any intention to hurt Denise, claiming the spray bottle of bleach was actually a bottle of water he was using to mist up her window to throw her off and to hide an empty gun clip. One week later, Brian appeared in court drenched in tears, but Denise begged that the judge refuse him bail for her and her daughter's safety. The judge agreed. Brian pleaded no contest, and his sentencing went ahead. Sixteen months later, in December 2017, Denise read an Emotional Victim Impact Statement asking for Brian to be penalised for assaulting her.

'We all have the right to feel secure and safe, and he stole it from me,' she said, with a victim advocate at her side. 'It comes down to my life or his, and I am asking you to choose mine.'[6]

She wanted Brian sentenced to life in prison for the crimes he had committed, but what she did not know was that just two months earlier, in October 2017, prosecutors had approached Brian. Florida law dictates that married couples are not required to testify against one another in court. Still, Denise and Brian's divorce had been officially finalised in May of that year, which meant the two were no longer protected by spousal privilege.

Not one to kick a gift horse in the mouth, the prosecutors presented Brian with an offer: tell the truth about what happened to Mike Williams, and not only would they provide full immunity for any charges relating to that case, but they would also void any potential life sentence for Denise's kidnapping.

At this point, it has been seventeen years since Jerry Michael Williams had gone missing, and finally, the answers started to pool out of Brian.

It all started during a double date night out between Brian, Kathy, Mike and Denise in 1997, when the conversation took a turn to sex. Brian and Denise had known each other since preschool, and whilst he had never romantically thought of her, the conversation sparked an attraction that Brian felt was mutual. The two couples went to a concert in October of that year. While Mike and Kathy went to park the car, Denise and Brian kissed for the first time. Later that night, after the couple returned home, Brian and Denise spoke on the phone for hours about everything under the sun, including their desires, and eventually, it led to phone sex. After which, a full-blown affair ensued.

They would rendezvous at hotels, public places, and sometimes Mike and Denise's house while Mike was at work. Sometimes, when Mike and Denise went out of town for one of Mike's business trips, Brian would follow them and spend time with Denise while Mike was at a conference. Things continued like this for years, and Brian kept having his cake and eating it. He said he had a good wife and a good kid, and Denise on the side. But Denise was unhappy in her marriage to Mike. The two fought constantly and hadn't had sex since Denise was pregnant.

Why don't they just get a divorce? Well, it wasn't an option for Denise. Not only did it go against her religious beliefs, she was worried she would lose full custody of her daughter. Denise also had her image to think about.

She was concerned that leaving Mike would affect her public image. As Brian later remarked, it is better to be a rich widow than a poor divorcee.

Denise and Brian wanted to be together fully, and although Brian could not pinpoint precisely who had brought it up, they started discussing ways to get Mike out of the picture. Staging a robbery at work, for example, but they ruled that out, knowing a full investigation would ensue. Another option was for both couples to go on a boating trip, which ended in a fatal accident that only Brian and Denise would survive. Whilst Brian didn't tell Denise at the time, he didn't want anything to happen to Kathy. He no longer wanted to be married to her, but that didn't mean he meant her harm.

Since Mike was making good money, Brian encouraged him to apply for a new life insurance policy through his father's financial planning company. On paper, it just looked like a friendly exchange of advice from one friend to another. Mike already had a $500,000 policy with another provider. He figured he could let that one lapse in exchange for a $1 million policy set up by the Winchesters. He didn't know that Denise planned on continuing to pay the premiums on the existing $500,000 policy so that, too, would remain active. Brian's fantasy is that he and Denise will live happily ever after with a lot of money.

During this time, Mike and Brian remained close friends and were on a hunting trip together when Mike suddenly walked into deep mud. It sucked him up like quicksand. Brian used significant force to pull him out of the bottomless mud pit. Had Mike been alone, there was a high chance he would have drowned. That's when Mike had the million-dollar idea. *This would be a great way to make Mike disappear.* He could lure Mike to an isolated spot on a lake, making sure he was wearing his waders; all Brian had to do was push him overboard and as soon as Mike hit the water, the waders would do all the work for him.

Denise liked this idea. Brian said it sat well with her because she could almost convince herself that it really was a tragic accident. But time was of the essence as Mike wanted to make some lifestyle changes.

He was talking about a new job, relocating out west with his family, or him and Denise trying for another baby. Whilst he had no idea about the affair, he knew something was going on with Denise. He confided in Brian that cash had been disappearing from his account, and he was worried that Denise might have something to do with it. Could she be doing drugs? Brian had to bite his tongue because he knew Denise was using that money on their trips.

Mike also voiced his frustration to Brian about their lack of sex life, and he hoped their upcoming wedding anniversary would be a chance to rekindle that spark, so Denise wanted to act fast. She didn't want to go on the trip, let alone reject Mike's advances and get into another fight with him. It was also only a matter of time before Mike noticed those old life insurance policy premiums being deducted from his checking account.

Slowly, the puzzle fell into place; all Brian and Denise needed were solid alibis. He planned a hunting trip with his father-in-law that morning, and Denise would use the landline sporadically so that people knew she was in.

On Friday night, 15 December, Brian took Kathy to a concert in Downtown Tallahassee. He encouraged her to drink as much as possible, hoping that she would sleep soundly when they got home and wake up late the next morning.

Brian woke before dawn, and Kathy was still fast asleep. He quickly snuck off to meet Mike at a gas station near the Iten Highway. Brian had told Mike they were going to a special hunting spot where they were denied their waders to ensure nothing could link the two of them together. He also told Mike that his phone wasn't charged conveniently, so he could not call him for any reason. Mike was none the wiser.

He met Brian as planned, just as they had done countless other hunting trips, and the two friends reached out to Lake Seminole in their respective vehicles. Once they reached Stump Field and headed out on the water, Brian waited until they were in the deepest part to put his plan into action.

Brian pushed him overboard when Mike stood up, but things quickly went askew. Mike managed to remove his hunting jacket and waders, meaning he wouldn't be dragged down, so not knowing what to do, he picked up his twelve-gauge shotgun and shot Mike directly in the head.

In a state of shock, Brian dragged Mike's body to the shore and loaded it into the back of his vehicle. He then pushed Mike's boat back out onto the water. Brian sped home, dismantling his shotgun as he drove, scattering the pieces out of the window. At one point, a highway patrol officer parked next to him at a red light but did not suspect a thing. When Brian arrived home, Kathy was still asleep, so he snuck into bed beside her while Mike's body lay waiting in his trunk.

Brian called his father-in-law, pretending to have overslept and missed the hunting trip, hoping that phone records would further solidify the alibi. Then, he drove to Walmart, where he purchased a tarp and a shovel.

He drove to a quick location, ten miles from his home, dug a shallow hole and buried Mike's body. After that, he thoroughly washed his car and assumed the role of a worried friend when his father called to say that Mike was missing.

As for the accusation that the waders had been planted in the water six months later, Brian denied this. He couldn't explain why they had taken so long to surface.

Brian never told Denise the truth about what happened, and she never asked. They lay low for as long as possible, waiting for an appropriate amount of time before Brian ended his marriage with Kathy. Only years later, when they felt things had well and truly died down, did Brian and Denise go public with what they pretended to be their new relationship. They agreed to never tell another soul what happened to Mike, no matter the pressure they were under.

Once Denise and Brian married, Brian felt somewhat safe in the lie they were living, given that they would be protected by spousal privilege, but the pressure came to a boil when their relationship started to fall apart in 2012. They both became increasingly paranoid and would often pat each other down before they talked about anything serious in case the other was wearing a wire. By the time Denise filed for divorce four years later, Brian was convinced she was going to talk, paranoia at its peak; he broke into Denise's car in the early hours of 5 August 2016 and waited until she climbed behind the wheel.

After confessing, Brian led investigators to where he had buried Mike. A specialist team was brought in to excavate the area as delicately as possible; it was no easy feat. Eventually, near the muddled dirt slope that acted as a makeshift boat ramp, they found Mike William's remains.

Brian Winchester was sentenced to twenty years in prison for the armed kidnapping of his ex-wife. Cheryl Williams was disappointed with the result, especially considering that she had lived without knowing where her son was for seventeen years and not having that closure while Mike had been free. But one thing for sure was that she did not want Denise to get away with it. Whilst she might not have pulled the trigger, she killed Mike, and she wanted her to pay for it.

Meanwhile, investigators continued building their case against Denise. Although Brian's confession was damning, prosecutors had to convince the grand jury that Denise had been involved in the murder plot all along. Their best idea was to prove that Brian and Denise were in a relationship long before Mike was murdered.

Police records revealed that when Mike was still alive, Brian's car had been reported as abandoned in a church parking lot close to William's home. When asked about this, Brian admitted he used to park his car there before walking the back streets to visit Denise. So that no one would see him toing and froing from the house. When police had contacted the Winchester home to inquire about the abandoned vehicle, Kathy picked up the call.

Brian had told Kathy he was out of town on a trip, so the suspicion crept in that he had gone to see Denise. Kathy had always suspected something was going on beneath the surface. Regardless, she maintained a close friendship with Denise over the years, but an odd phone call she received from Denise one week after Brian's arrest raised some red flags.

'Tell Brian's father to get a message to Brian that I'm not talking,' she said down the phone. Suspicious as to what this meant, Kathy agreed with the police to covertly record her phone conversations with Denise.

In one call, Kathy told Denise she had been subpoenaed concerning the charges against Brian. She was worried Mike's disappearance would be brought up.

She revealed to Denise, 'I've always just pretended like I don't know anything, and I do know–'

'–What do you know?'[7]

Kathy told Denise she knew about the affair and that she regretted not saying anything to Mike because he could still have been alive. Denise pressed Kathy to elaborate, but she didn't deny or confess anything to investigators. Her emotionless response served as further proof that she had been in on the murder plan.

On Tuesday, 8 May 2018, six law enforcement officers gathered outside Denise's office at Florida State University and placed the forty-eight-year-old under arrest. A grand jury had indicted her for first-degree murder, conspiracy to commit first-degree murder and accessory after the fact. Denise said nothing and stared straight ahead as she was let out in handcuffs and into a waiting patrol car.

Denise Williams pleaded not guilty to all charges, and her trial commenced in December 2018, almost 18 years to the day since Mike was killed. The defence maintained that Denise had never known the truth about what happened to Mike and that she had nothing to do with Brian Winchester's murder plot.

They argued that Brian was bitter about the failed marriage and was essentially trying to take Denise down with him. The jury was urged not to believe the word of a self-confessed murderer and kidnapper, with Denise's lawyer stating there was no tangible or physical evidence tying Denise Williams to this crime. Their view was that all the jury had to go on was the word of a murderer, and they were going to have to decide if they believed him.

During cross-examination, the defence tried to cast doubt on the duration of Brian and Denise's affair, questioning how it could have gone on for so long without anyone finding out. Brian's defence was Denise's intelligence. The defence responded, claiming that Brian was obsessed with Denise, and his response was they were best friends, Bonnie and Clyde, partners in crime. They were obsessed *with each other*.

The defence asked Brian if Denise was with him when he shot Mike, and he shrugged as he admitted that she wasn't, but he added she was in his head, behind him.

After four days of testimony, the jury deliberated for eight hours before returning their verdict.

Guilty on all counts.

Unbeknownst to investigators, the day Denise was arrested was Denise and Mike's daughter's 19th birthday. Cheryl always maintained that losing her granddaughter was one of the most painful aspects of the whole ordeal. Cheryl had posted a birthday message for her in the local newspaper every year, hoping she knew her grandmother was thinking of her. At Denise's sentencing, Cheryl told the judge not only did Denise kill my son, but she stole her granddaughter for her entire life. Her granddaughter was raised in a house with the murderers of her father while being denied the love of her father's family. She was told that Grandma Cheryl was crazy and would hurt her. No amount of prison time would bring Mike back to Cheryl, and she didn't know if she would ever have her granddaughter back in her life again.

When Mike Williams went missing on 15 December 2000, he did not meet the standard statistics for people who go missing. He was a well-standing businessman, a devoted husband and father. Still, investigators jested that he was sitting in the Bahamas just relaxing because the leading theory is that when someone has it all, they don't just go missing. They leave on their own. And to that end, what resources would law enforcement use if that was the case? It was only because Mike's mother never gave up that they realised Mike was a victim of foul play.

It's strange because if Mike was a woman and Denise was a man, we would have immediately thought that Mike had been killed for money and revenge. It would have been the 'husband did it' trope in real life, but this had not been applied at first in this case, and foul play was never considered. However, you could apply Occam's Razor in two different ways. You could use both sides if you will. On one side, you could say the simplest explanation was that Mike fell into the lake and drowned, but the other side states that when the evidence is stacked and measured up, in this case, the husband did do it. It was just a different one.

As of 2019, Denise has not faced additional insurance fraud charges or paid restitution to the state for collecting $1.75 million from Mike's three life insurance policies. Prosecutors dropped the charges as part of a settlement agreement blessed by Cheryl and Nick, which shifted Denise's assets to Mike's daughter, Ainsley Williams.

'Mike would have wanted her to have this,' Cheryl confirmed, 'Michael would have wanted her to be taken care of for the rest of her life.'

The assets given to Ainsley Williams include four pieces of Tallahassee real estate valued at about $877,000, including her home on Centennial Oaks Circle, purchased by her parents as a baby.

Currently, Cheryl and Anslee remain estranged.[8]

Chapter Ten

The Disappearance of the McStay Family

When googling 'the likelihood of families going missing,' the results were quite slim. The results comprise vital statistics and figures about missing persons and children. Almost nothing about entire families. It may be rare, but it does not mean it never happens.

The research confirmed that certain people are more at risk of going missing than others, possibly because of homelessness, mental health issues, and problems at home, including relationship breakdown and financial struggles.[1]

Only one of these scenarios applied to the McStay Family.

As the cold bled into the February evening in 2010, Joseph and Summer McStay and their two sons, 4-year-old Gianni and 3-year-old Joseph Junior, left their snug family home in suburban San Diego Court, Fallbrook. Piling into their Isuzu Trooper, they left behind two dogs and two bowls of popcorn untouched. A lamp was knocked over in a bedroom, and the coffee was still in the pot. Why would they leave the house in such an active state?

Joseph McStay was a laidback surfer and an outgoing, chatty businessman. Summer McStay was a woman who was unafraid to say what was on her mind. And they both loved their two sons dearly. Then why was 4 February 2010, the last day the McStays were seen? Why have their bank accounts been withdrawn and their mobile phones and emails quiet since then? Just mere days after Joe Junior had turned three.

It is put best by Deputy District Attorney Sean Daughtery, who said, 'How does a family of four disappear off the face of the earth? How does a family of four, a husband who is running a business, a mom who is raising her two kids, fixing up a house they bought just recently, how do they just disappear?'[2]

How indeed?

On 10 February, Joseph's father got a call from a D Kavanaugh, which he deleted because why would he answer a call from someone he didn't know? But then he got an email from the same person. He asks his son Michael, who was able to shed some enlightenment, 'You know what person, Dad? It's Dan, the hacker.'

Suddenly, it clicked: Dan Kavanagh used to work with Joseph then and presided over their website. He used to get a particular percentage of the sales made online. But why was he calling Joseph's dad?

Michael called him, and Dan hadn't heard from Joseph in days. Joseph was not one to leave his debts unpaid, but why wasn't he calling back? By Monday, Joseph's father was duly upset and thinking the worst, so he asked Michael to go and check on them. Michael was the only one who lived nearby, so it made sense, but he declined, stating he was too busy. He thought maybe they had gone on an impromptu family trip. Perhaps there had been an emergency on Summer's side of the family, so they left in such a hurry. But does that mean they couldn't take five to answer their families' frantic calls? Something wasn't adding up.

But Dan wasn't the only one looking for Joseph; Joseph's best friend, Chase Merrit, was. Chase Merrit was Joseph's business associate for his company 'Earth Inspired Products', which built decorative fountains. Chase was known as his welder. He would make anything Joseph designed. And they grew closer than business associates. They became very close friends, intertwined in each other's lives, talked fifteen times daily, and had dinners at each other's houses.

On 13 February, Michael travelled to the McStay residence and climbed in through an open window in the back, hoping for some clue as to what might have happened. Michael did not find any family at home; their two dogs were in the backyard, and the house was in disarray. After some convincing from Chase, on 15 February, Michael phoned the San Diego County Sheriff's Department and filed a missing person's report.

Officers arrived at the home and requested a search warrant when Michael let Deputy Tingley inside. Tingley didn't see any blood or broken items. There were no signs of an evident struggle. The house was empty.

The two men searched every room and closet, but no one needed help or bodies.

This missing person's case was going to be escalated, and although it looked like no crime had occurred, Deputy Tingley alerted the homicide division.

It is incredibly unusual for an entire family to be missing for an estimated eleven days now, so law enforcement moved into action. The house went into lockdown, and additional units were called in. The Sheriff's Office knocked on neighbours' doors to see if anyone saw something suspicious or if home surveillance cameras could have captured any clues. But, of course, the investigation ran into some issues.

According to authorities, one of the Mcstay's neighbours gave a small portion of her camera footage but would not hand it all over, later testifying that if they took her cameras, she wouldn't feel safe in her home. This was less than ideal, but everyone in the neighbourhood felt pretty on edge after learning about the missing family.

Homicide detective Troy DuGal, a twenty-three-year veteran on the force, headed to the scene to take over. After surveying the home, he experienced Lebensblick, a vignette into the Mcstay's life. Freshly painted walls with blue painter's tape still attached. A mattress on the master bedroom floor instead of a bed. Rotting bananas and a carton of eggs on the counter. Two children-sized bowls almost full with popcorn were left on the futon as if their snack time had suddenly been interrupted. Other than that, no inclination as to where the McStay's could be.

As the investigation continued, authorities discovered that the family's Isuzu Trooper was found abandoned and had been towed on 8 February 2010, from a shopping centre near the Mexico border. Could they have just gone on an impromptu holiday? Leaving the house in such disarray? DuGal knew, though, that people frequently illegally parked in these parking lots where the vehicle was. Could they have illegally parked there to walk across the border?[3]

At this point, Troy was unsure if they had a homicide case, but they knew they had a missing person's case. He was more concerned because their children had gone, and he didn't have a reasonable explanation. If the adults were fighting, it's a very traditional domestic issue. Two adults fight; one runs away, and the other goes chasing. The family may not know what's going on. He thinks of these hypotheticals from a missing person's aspect, but he also keeps the idea of homicide as a possibility.

Detective DuGal was trying to gather as much information as he could. He would later testify that he had been working on the case nonstop, even juggling this case with others.

What doesn't help is that the department resources were spread thin following another high-profile murder in the area where a teenager was raped and murdered while out jogging. Dugal testified that he only slept about five hours a night. It is vital to note the actual humanity behind the investigators. When you watch true crime shows, you always see the investigators use their minds, but I forget that there are human beings who need food, sleep and have a life. The lack of resources could end in human error, but the odds are just out of their control.

Investigators have been trained and have extensive authority to find missing persons, to determine how they died, and to determine the culprit. They can make crucial decisions that profoundly impact individuals' lives. It is almost like they play God.

Regardless, DuGal started interviewing people in the McStay family circle, from relatives to business associates. According to his testimony in court, he received some disturbing news. Joseph's mother, Susan Blake, had gone over to the McStay's house and was cleaning it, straightening it up. While people handle fear and panic in their own ways, including cleaning, Susan really should not have cleaned a house and gotten rid of piles of potential evidence. She bleached the place, putting things in order in time for her son, who she was sure would return soon. Michael even went to the house and took Joseph's computer from his office.

Michael later testified that he took his brother's computer with the intent of turning over financial records to the detectives, but he didn't have a power cord, *so he couldn't even run the machine.*

Detective DuGal was learning that the family might have been disposing of crucial evidence whilst he was seeking a search warrant for the residence. Stating that the case was off to a bad start is an understatement, as it faced significant challenges from the outset.

DuGal tried to tactfully convey to Susan that she should refrain from touching the house and that she needed to have Michael return the computer. The family was unaware of his efforts to obtain a search warrant for entry. He wanted to be discreet lest he cause unnecessary alarm.

He knew obtaining a warrant from a judge would be difficult because he had to prove that a crime had been committed at the residence or in their cars. Since there were no bodies in the house, this was going to prove difficult. And if the McStays were dead, their bodies hadn't shown up as the investigation continued.

At this point, where was the family of four after fifteen days? They surely would have contacted by now. Even the theory that they had gone on holiday was starting to appear implausible.

DuGal's interviews hadn't been very fruitful, but that was to be expected. When dealing with a missing person's case, when their loved ones do not believe they are missing, so they only talk about the good things, the positive anecdotes. Their business was great, they were wealthy, and the kids were a joy. DuGal wants to know the bad stuff, the dark underbelly of it. He wants to know who doesn't like them and who owes them money. The dark things would be uncovered over time.

He searched the Trooper and the house, but the house already looked different from the prior one. It was cleaner, losing some of that 'lived-in' feeling. Clothes had been picked up, and scattered newspapers had been picked up. The eggs, popcorn and bananas have been put away, too.

Detective DuGal scoured for evidence – blood, signs of forced entry, anything that could shed light. Yet, all he discovered were a child's beanie, a gaming controller, and a leash atop a circular wooden table. During the trial, the prosecution scrutinized photographs of that very table, pinpointing minuscule red droplets resembling blood splatter. It was something the detective had overlooked. DuGal couldn't definitively identify what lay at the bottom of that photograph when he faced questioning at trial, leaving an unsettling pit in his stomach. Despite his profound knowledge of blood splatter, uncertainty clouded his testimony.

While searching the residence, officials retrieved potential evidence, including computers, a thumb drive, cameras, checks, cell phones, and records. Cadaver dogs, specialized in detecting human body decomposition, thoroughly examined the backyard. However, additional excavation measures, such as tearing up the carpet, were withheld at this stage. The search prioritized locating a crime scene and evidence; further actions, such as more extensive chemical testing or physical alterations like tearing up the carpet and cutting walls, were deferred until conclusive evidence was identified.

The investigation identified Joseph's and Summer's last outgoing calls from their phones were on 4 February, one of them to Chase Merrit. The McStay's also had not used their bank.

DuGal sent a sergeant and another detective down to the US-Mexico border to inquire with Immigration, Customs and Border Patrol to find any camera that records on either side of the border and to collect all video from 8 February 2010, for future review.

A video was discovered depicting what seemed to be two adults accompanied by two small children. Extracted from the San Ysidro port of entry on the exact day the vehicle was towed, the footage suggested a family of four strolling casually across the border into Mexico. While this finding provided a glimmer of hope, Mike expressed reservations due to the subpar video quality, hindering a definitive identification. In fact, Mike noted that the individual in the video exhibited a walking style vastly different from that of his brother. The National Centre for Missing and Exploited Children collaborated in analysing the video.

This was a complex process because imagine how many people walked across that border that day alone. At night, you would have to watch every person walking across that border and decipher the body language from the pixels. The video was low quality as it is. You don't see the faces of the individuals, and even so, they are walking away from the camera.

The National Centre for Missing and Exploited Children returned, but the quality made it a dead end. So, DuGal moved to the next potential motive, Earth Inspired Products, the business Joseph ran.

Joseph sold customised water fountains and waterfalls, high-end features, sometimes costing thousands of dollars. They were shipped all over the world, including Saudi Arabia. It was a successful business, and this is where his welder, Charles (Chase) Merrit, came in.

Chase sounded the initial alarm to Joseph's mother on 9 February, concerned that he couldn't reach him. He even went to McStay's empty house to leave food and water out for the dogs left behind. He was the one who wanted Michael to call the police.

Fast forward to 17 February, detectives met with Chase for a lengthy three-hour recorded interview about Chase's interactions with Joseph and Summer, leading to their disappearance. The last time Chase saw Joseph, in fact, the last time anyone saw Joseph and/or Summer, was 4 February.

Chase and Joseph met at Chick-fil-A to exchange cheques; detectives went to the fast-food joint, but two weeks after that meeting, the video surveillance was gone, so they couldn't independently verify what Chase had said.

But he was helpful in other ways. He provided a lot of insight into the McStay family, from tensions with Joseph's wife, Summer, to Joseph's business associate, who might have had an axe to grind.

He tried to be careful with the words he used to describe Summer and instead described Joseph as 'pussy whipped'. He even went far enough to say that nobody around Joseph liked Summer; they didn't want him to marry her because she was 'difficult.' But nothing concerning stood out to DuGal; instead, he moved on to Chase's finances.[4]

He openly acknowledged grappling with financial hardships, revealing that the business had been in an economic downturn for six to seven months. During that period, sales had almost come to a halt, posing a severe threat to the business's financial stability. However, there has been a recent upturn, and the outlook looks promising.

When discussing this case with my work colleagues, I mentioned the McStay family case and likely scenarios, and what I found very interesting was the immediate response of my colleague who asked, 'Did anyone benefit from them going missing?' It's a good idea to keep that in consideration.

Chase didn't think the family went to Mexico, and he was asked point blank if he was involved in the family's disappearance. He emphatically said no. He had nothing to gain from it. Chase is a builder; he can't maintain the business without Joseph. Chase and Dan tried to pick up the pieces and run the business until Joseph returned. Chase had never met Dan in person, but he knew Dan was technology-savvy.

While Chase verified that Joseph didn't have adversaries, he acknowledged a rift between Joseph and Dan. Joseph was in the process of paying Dan $50,000 to acquire his share and still owed him approximately $2000. The arrangement involved Dan transitioning from a partner to solely managing the site.

Chase sensed that Dan was not a person to be trifled with; he held the power to shut down the site, which was the leverage Dan employed during conflicts with Joseph. This dynamic prompted Joseph's desire to buy out Dan.

Chase was an ex-felon and had a probation violation out for his arrest, something investigators were fully aware of. Although he had never been convicted of a violent crime before, he had served time for receiving stolen property, burglary, petty theft and other crimes. Detectives assured Chase he would not be arrested for the outstanding warrant if he worked with them. To them, finding the McStay's was more important than Chase's legal issues.

One of the detectives pointed out that Chase used the past tense to talk about Joseph during the interview, maybe a Freudian slip of the tongue? Or just an accident? The detectives must not have thought much of it because Chase wasn't made to submit a DNA sample.

Later in March, a month after Joseph's disappearance, Susan, Chase, Dan, Michael, and Patrick, Joseph's father, began meeting to keep the business afloat. These were tense negotiations, ending with Susan, Patrick and Mike being estranged for a while.

Susan began writing Chase cheques from her personal account, which she felt was an act of love for Joseph to support his business, so it was still there when he returned home. But she was never reimbursed, something she would later testify in court.

There were two meetings and a frequent occurrence was Dan and Chase yelling at each other, not bickering, *yelling*, so Susan stood up and said, 'If my son loses his business, so be it. I need to find my family,' and she left.

At this point the McStay's disappearance had garnered national attention, with Michael appearing on 'Nancy Grace' multiple times and

Detective DuGal flying into Washington and appearing on 'America's Most Wanted.' He was getting flooded with tips, including from psychics and mediums who wanted to weigh in on the case. But nothing substantial was revealed, no arrests were made, and the McStay's were never found.

In April 2010, the case was turned over to the FBI, but no answers emerged for more than three years, until 11 November 2013.

John Bluth, a Napa Valley dirt biker, was spending that Veteran's Day dirt biking. Something caught his eye as he went off-road near the county landfill, about 100 miles from the McStay's house and less than a mile from the freeway.

A small white object.

It was a bone.

Later, he would discover that it was a part of a child's human skull.

He put his bike on the side stand and looked at the object. He thought it might have been human, so he returned to his bike and called the Sheriff's department.

Dr Alexis Grey, a forensic anthropologist, was celebrating her wedding anniversary at home when she got the call from the San Bernardino County Sheriff's Office. She went to the desolate scene in the middle of the desert, where she saw an adult's tibia and femur lying in the sand.

The Sheriff's Office set up a command post and began to excavate, where they discovered two shallow graves.

The partial remains of the four McStay family members had been found.

Joseph and Joe Junior were buried together in a grave that animals had dug up, consuming some of their remains.

Summer and Gianni were buried about ten inches into the sand in the second grave. In one of the graves were skull fragments and dark hair.

In Summer's burial site, the sheriff's office recovered soiled and worn black pants tangled with a woman's white underwear, suggesting they had been hastily removed. Alongside these, detectives uncovered additional items from the gravesite – a kitty backpack, a fragment of a robe, an empty cell phone case, a diaper, a torn bra, and a sledgehammer bearing traces of paint matching that of the family's residence. Despite the passage of time, faint remnants of two sets of tire tracks leading to the graves remained visible.

Dr Chanikarn Changsri was the chief forensic pathologist for the San Bernadino's Coroner's Division. It was her job to conduct an autopsy, to look at the history and circumstances to determine the cause and manner of death. Dr Changsri has undertaken alone 400 to 500 autopsies annually. She knew what she was doing.

She studied the partial remains of Joseph, Summer and the two little boys that had arrived in three boxes and one body bag. On 14 November 2013, she ruled the manner of death as homicide.

Joseph McStay was the most preserved of his family members; his body was encased in a woven fabric. His ribs were broken, there was an open hole in the back of his head, plus other fractures on his skull. His skull had been hit at least four times. The back of his right leg was fractured. He was wrapped in a white electrical cord. Dr Changsri ruled the cause of death as blunt force trauma.

Summer McStay's skull had been shattered into multiple pieces, her jaw was broken in several places, and her skull had been struck at least six times, and this was determined as her cause of death. Dr Changsri could not determine if Summer had been raped because there was no soft tissue left in the vaginal area of the remains.

Three-year-old Joe Jr's death was undetermined.

Four-year-old Gianni was killed by multiple blunt force injuries to the head. He received at least six strikes right around the time of his death.

Looking at the damage to the bones, Dr Changsri believed the three-pound sledgehammer found in the grave was the murder weapon that had bludgeoned the entire family.

Following the discovery of the bodies, the San Bernardino County Sheriff's Department, led by Sean Dougherty, assumed control of the investigation. With access to more significant resources, they swiftly deployed them, yielding intriguing breakthroughs starting in early February, just before the family's disappearance. Employing a process of elimination, the investigators initially focused on Chase Merrit, the last known individual to have seen Joseph alive.

The newly unsealed search warrants in the quadruple-murder case said detectives analysed the family's vehicle and collected DNA swabs. When detectives looked at this DNA evidence again in 2014, criminalists matched the DNA collected from the Trooper to Merritt. His DNA was collected from the steering wheel, the shifter and the radio.

Detectives reviewed transcripts of prior interviews with Merritt, who had passed a lie detector test when initially questioned in February 2010. Upon review, his words sent up a red flag. He used the past tense to describe Joseph, saying he 'was my best friend' years before the bodies would be found.[5]

Merritt confirmed that on 14 February 2010, the day the family disappeared, Merritt and Joseph met for lunch at a Chick-fil-A restaurant in Rancho Cucamonga for a business meeting. Just to go over financials according to Merritt.

However, he would also tell investigators that he had been the last to see Joseph. Which is an odd comment to make. How is anyone certain that they were the last to see their best friend alive?

Both instances raised investigators' suspicions, but another glaring clue would ultimately put Chase at the centre of the investigation.

Investigators gained access to Joseph's online ledger systems and his QuickBooks records. They found that on 1 February, three days before his disappearance, Joseph's QuickBooks was accessed, but not from any of the computers at the McStay house.

Joseph had just sent an email to Chase saying that Joseph had overpaid him, and the total owed to him now was $42,000. About forty-five minutes after receiving that email, someone entered Joseph's QuickBooks and added Charles Merritt as a vendor. The name was added in all lowercase. Doughtery said that he would capitalise the first letter whenever Joseph would enter a vendor.

Two cheques were then created for $2,500 each. They were deleted, meaning they wouldn't appear on the ledger. The next day, Doughtery said someone went into Joseph's QuickBooks again, not from the McStay's computers and two more cheques were added to Charles Merrit. They were, again, printed and then deleted.

This is something Joseph had never done before.

That same day, one of the cheques was cashed at the bank. Joseph also made some calls to his bank and then Chase. Then he signed into his

QuickBooks and signed out. Two minutes later, after he signed out, he called the bank again. It looks like he caught on to what Chase had done.

The next set of interactions was recovered via cell phone towers.

Doughtery said that after Joseph called Chase between 12.52 pm and 1.00 pm. There were twelve frantic phone calls, primarily from Chase to his wife. She called him back at 1.00 pm.

After the time the meeting was supposed to occur at Chick-fil-A, Joseph called Chase seven times. The longest call lasted over two minutes.

By 5.48 pm, Joseph's phone had returned southbound near his residence. Following this, Chase's phone ceased connecting to towers, likely turned off or in aeroplane mode. At 7.56 pm, someone accessed Joseph's QuickBooks via the McStay's home computer, manipulating a lowercase $4000 check to Charles Merrit, subsequently deleting it and logging out. At 8.28 pm, Joseph's phone registered a call to Chase, although Chase's phone was inactive then. At 9.28 pm, Chase contacted his wife, his phone connecting to a tower just south of Rancho Cucamonga, which became untraceable until 7.30 am. At this point, the McStay's had disappeared.

On 5 February, an additional four checks amounting to $12,855 were generated, dated back to the 4th, with two made out to Charles Merrit. These entries were erased on the same day.

The following day, on 6 February, Chase's cell phone signal registered with towers situated close to the location where the bodies were eventually discovered.

By 8 February, the McStay family's vehicle was located at the border.

Adding to the concern, an unsettling call was recalled by a QuickBooks customer service representative, allegedly from an individual claiming to be 'Joseph McStay.' This person sought complete deletion of the account and its associated data. However, Hanke clarified that the phone utilized for this call belonged to Merritt, not Joseph.

Due to the absence of the required passcode, the customer service representative couldn't fulfil the deletion request, leaving potentially incriminating information for investigators to uncover later.

Looking at the evidence, it isn't looking favourable for Chase. He not only had a motive to carry out the killings, it appeared he had the chance as well. Records from his cell phone indicated Merritt's presence in the desert, where the bodies were found, a mere two days after the family vanished. Investigators noted Merritt's upbringing in the region, highlighting his familiarity with the landscape.

On 5 November 2014, detectives from the SDSO arrested Merritt in connection with the deaths of the McStay family after discovering that his DNA had been recovered from their car. His arrest was announced on 7 November 2014.

The trial was delayed because Merrit repeatedly fired his attorneys or attempted to represent himself. By February 2016, he had gone through five attorneys.

The trial would not officially begin until 7 January 2019, because Merrit's attorneys tried to file a notion on 7 April 2018, arguing that Joseph's business and accounting evidence were hearsay and therefore inadmissible. Their concerns were that only Joseph himself could validate their accuracy. Ultimately, the judge determined that a foundation could be laid to establish checks were written and cashed. However, proving Merritt was indebted to Joseph McStay could be problematic if no witnesses could be called to testify about that.[6]

When the trial finally began, both sides made their opening statements.

Prosecutors alleged that Merritt had a gambling problem and killed the McStay family for financial gain. Defence attorneys continued along that trajectory as the trial progressed, consistently contesting the prosecution's case. They conveyed to the jury that the evidence would indicate a lack of proof regarding Merrit's presence in Fallbrook during the McStay's disappearance, and there was no physical evidence linking him to the burial locations.

The case's narratives are vastly divergent. Prosecutors assert the family was fatally assaulted in their Fallbrook residence, alleging a beating as the cause of death. Conversely, the defence disputes this, asserting the absence of any blood evidence at home despite indications from the victims' remains suggesting a sledgehammer attack. The defence maintains that the family perished in the desert where their bodies were discovered.

The nail in the coffin, however, was the QuickBooks records. The evidence suggested that Chase Merritt was financially manipulating and using Joseph, who happened to disappear when he confronted Chase about it? It doesn't seem like mere chance.

The next nail in the coffin was Joseph's mother giving Chase money to keep the business afloat, and she testified that he never gave it back.

The prosecutors theorised that Merrit assassinated the family for financial gain and that he and Joseph had a falling out on 4 February due to Joseph finding out. After Chase's phone went off the grid, he killed the McStay family in their home, took their bodies and buried them at the grave site later on 6 February. Then, on 8 February, he took their car to the border.

Initially, the theory appears airtight, but certain aspects do not align. The absence of blood within the home makes it highly improbable that the McStays were killed there, save for that potential speck found on the photo frame. Additionally, there were no reports from neighbours indicating any disturbances.

Furthermore, the absence of blood in the truck raises questions; blood would likely be present on both the assailant and the victims because it moves. It should have been evidence in the vehicle. Could Chase have executed this alone? Transporting and burying four bodies in the desert seems implausible. The pieces simply don't fit together.

Chase's defence attempted to implement DNA transfer as the theory for Chase's DNA being in the car; they stated Joseph shook Chase's hand, then he touched the steering wheel, then the gearshift in the centre console, which is why it was present in the car. He was also excluded as the contributor of the DNA on the items recovered in the graves.

Additionally, why would Chase kill Joseph for money when Earth Inspired Products had lined up such lucrative orders over the next several years, with a trajectory to make the pair millionaires?

So if Chase was, in fact, innocent, then who did kill the McStay family?

According to 'Two Shallow Graves', a documentary series produced for ID by Red Marble Media, many people could have been the assailant.[7]

One was Summer's ex-boyfriend, who had sent her an email just months before the family's disappearances telling her he would 'love her forever.' He lived near the family and had been previously arrested for threatening a neighbour and her daughter.

There was also the new husband of Joseph's ex-wife, a man with a history of violence, who had allegedly threatened to 'muzzle' Summer and beat up her husband.

And then, there was Dan Kavanagh.

During the investigation, Tracey Riccobene, Daniel Kavanagh's ex-girlfriend, went to investigators and defence to give a statement.

She entered the room with an agitated demeanour, her limbs in constant motion, exuding a palpable nervousness.

She wasted no time asserting a bold claim: they had apprehended the wrong individual, arguing that Dan orchestrated the framing. Before this, it was established that Dan had sought compensation for his algorithmic contribution to Joseph's business but faced resistance when Joseph considered a buyout instead. Could this financial disagreement be construed as a potential motive?

Tracey recounted Dan's confession to her, detailing a harrowing incident where he held one of the boys at knifepoint, coercing the family out of their home. He subsequently forced Joseph and the boys to leave while he raped Summer. Upon their return, Dan purportedly committed the atrocious murders. Despite Tracey's unease and Dan's intimidation tactics, she felt compelled by duty to disclose this information regardless of the personal toll it might exact.

Again, there are a few holes in this narrative: are the prosecutors supposed to believe that Joseph and the boys left the house and didn't attempt to get help.

Also, Tracey's behaviour was abnormal, as in someone under the influence abnormal. So much so that Merrit's defence does not call her a witness, and the jury does not see her interview. But they do want to call Daniel to stand. But no one could find Dan for all five months of the trial.

Merrit's defence team wanted to put forward the idea that the best fitting profile of the murder of the McStay family was Dan, and the investigators wrongfully focused on Chase early on and failed to make a thorough investigation of other potential perpetrators. Dan among them.

After the family's disappearance, Kavanaugh approached Joseph McStay's mother and Merritt, and the three became involved in an effort, which also included Joseph McStay's half-brother Mike McStay, to keep Earth Inspired Products afloat until Joseph returned. Ultimately, Kavanaugh took well over $100,000 out of the business for himself and honed in on the company's ownership, eventually selling it in June 2011. The contract of the sale was never subpoenaed, nor were the terms found out. Seems like he had something to benefit from them disappearing.

However, Dan Kavanaugh allegedly claimed to have been in Hawaii during the time of the McStay family's disappearance and brutal murder. As the series disclosed, one of his girlfriends had validated the claims.

The defence meticulously seized every opportunity to delve into Kavanaugh's involvement. They probed the prosecution's witnesses about Kavanaugh's ties to Joseph McStay, the escalating conflict between them leading up to Joseph's demise due to commissions withheld from Kavanaugh for custom water projects. They highlighted Kavanaugh's swift takeover of Earth Inspired Products after the family's disappearance, diverting funds and ultimately claiming ownership and profits from its sale. The televised revelation on 'Two Shallow Graves' showcased Kavanaugh's confession to hacking Joseph's financial accounts long before his disappearance, supporting Chase's assertion that the switch in QuickBooks was to thwart Kavanaugh's hacking.

Despite Judge Smith's initial ruling restricting third-party culpability, the trial has evolved into a battleground for two theories – Merritt versus Kavanaugh – as potential perpetrators. Kavanaugh's whereabouts during the family's disappearance emerged as a pivotal trial point. While purchases and a ticket linked to Kavanaugh suggest he was in Hawaii, the absence of boarding passes and doubts about the credit card's possession by his then-girlfriend cast uncertainty on his alibi. Notably, investigators never verified Kavanaugh's claim of being in Hawaii. In the end, nothing further was followed up with Dan in the court case.

The court case presented an intricate challenge, heavily leaning toward implicating Chase. He had been the last known individual to see the victims before their disappearance, stood to benefit financially from their demise, and faced a multitude of damning factors. The premature house cleaning preceding the search warrant likely erased crucial evidence that could have vindicated him.

What's perplexing is the prosecution's relentless focus on Chase without considering other potential suspects. For instance, why wasn't Dan thoroughly investigated? Was all of the evidence procured against Merritt circumstantial?

The jury's decision and subsequent sentencing seemed predetermined, weighted heavily against Merritt. Despite the appearance of financial gain in the short term for Chase, Dan may have stood to gain more in the long run and should have, at the very least, been regarded as a witness. It felt as though he was given a pass, considering the circumstances.

Nonetheless, a tragic reality looms – the brutal demise of an entire family, their bodies left to nature's mercy in shallow graves, nearly impossible to reconstruct due to decomposition and animal interference. Their irreplaceable loss is a poignant reminder that a human tragedy lies behind the legal proceedings and evidential puzzles.

The re-examination of the case in the 2022 docuseries 'Two Shallow Graves' on Investigation Discovery sheds light on fresh suspects, witnesses, evidence, and theories. It offers an insight into the trial from both the defendant's and prosecutor's perspectives, seeking to unravel the complex layers of this haunting case.

Chapter Eleven

The Story of Michael Morton

S at in his windowless cell shared with another inmate, on 12 April 1987, Michael Morton wrote a letter. 'Your honour, I'm sure you remember me. I was convicted of murder in your court in February of this year.'

A small metal locker bolted to the wall contained the few remnants he still possessed from his previous life: a photograph of his son Eric when he was 3 years old, standing in the backyard of their house in Austin. The judge he is writing to is the one who will decide if he can see Eric ever again. 'I miss him terribly, knowing he has been asking about me. [...] I must reiterate my innocence. I did NOT kill my wife.'[1]

There is a common saying in true crime: it's always the husband. This is usually in jest, but this saying is founded upon unfortunate statistics. About 34% of the women killed in the U.S. in 2021 died at the hands of an intimate partner, according to the Bureau of Justice statistics. Whereas 6% of the men killed in the U.S. in 2021 died from intimate partner homicide.[2]

While it's essential to uphold the principle of 'innocent until proven guilty,' in Michael Morton's case, authorities focused solely on one suspect without exploring other leads. The presumption of innocence aims to ensure a fair trial for those accused, but how was this principle upheld in Michael Morton's situation?

Born 12 August 1954, Michael spent his earlier years moving between different towns as he watched his father service the oil patches across Southern California and Texas. By the time Michael was a junior in high school, his family had settled in Kilgore, Texas, before he left to attend Stephen F. Austin State University in Nacogdoches.

It was during a psychology course that Michael first met Christine Marie Fitzpatrick. Unlike Michael, who is often slower to warm to people,

Christine was friendly and unguarded, with long brown hair and bright blue eyes. She had disarming confidence.

In his memoir, Michael described seeing Christine for the first time in a vast classroom amphitheatre. He said 'she was standing several rows up from me, holding her books to her chest, talking with and taking the measure of my roommate. Luckily for me, he wasn't her type.'[3]

A few days later, Michael invited Christine to a party he was having at his apartment, and she said yes, and as they say, the rest was history.

They were often described as a passionate couple. Michael liked to rib Christine, and his sense of humour could be sarcastic and sometimes crude, sometimes going over what is acceptable. A running gag between them involved Michael calling out, 'Bitch, get me a beer!' – something they had once overheard a friend of a friend shout at his girlfriend.

Christine would respond by telling Michael to go screw himself.

Nevertheless, they were both very vocal when they argued and got everything out in the open. Probably because of their frankness with one another that kept their connection strong, so strong they married in 1979.

In 1981, the couple discovered they were pregnant with their first child, a girl. They chose the name Nicole and excitedly awaited the arrival of their baby daughter. When Christine was twenty-two weeks into her pregnancy, they went for a check-up, where they tragically learnt that the doctor could not find a heartbeat. They had lost their baby.

But hope would bloom two years later when Christine became pregnant for the second time, expecting a little boy. She reached her ninth month of pregnancy without serious complications, and she and Michael welcomed their son Eric into the world.

However, hours after giving birth, the new parents were informed that Eric had been born with a hole in his heart. Meaning he could not get enough oxygen. He also underwent surgery to repair an abnormality in his oesophagus the day he was born, but the Mortons were told that his heart couldn't be fixed until he was 3 years old or weighed thirty pounds. Operating sooner carried too much risk, but without the surgery, Eric would not live to see adulthood.

Embracing parenthood brings an immense shift; it's a sudden entrance of a pivotal force into your life – a responsibility to nurture, protect, and ensure the happiness and well-being of this new addition. It entails sleepless nights and chaotic days filled with cries, yet amidst these challenges, precious moments – the giggles, the first steps, the heartwarming gummy smiles – make this transformation worthwhile. Nonetheless, navigating this transition becomes significantly more challenging when coupled with medical complications.

Michael and Christine devoted themselves to caring for Eric. Their focus changed, and every moment of their lives was dominated by fear for him. The demands of his stringent medication schedule and the struggle to keep him alive.

The new parents lived in constant fear that if they missed a dosage or weren't paying enough attention, Eric would die. It is a mental deterrent to be under that much pressure, and it didn't bode well for their marriage.

The strain on the relationship became obvious. Nothing stayed below the surface for long, and Michael's wisecracks began to have a harder edge. He openly complained to friends that he and Christine were not having enough sex and that she needed to lose weight.

Despite the stress or mental strain Michael might have been under, his remarks were unacceptable, yet Christine chose to dismiss them. Ultimately, she held firm in the knowledge that Michael loved her, reciprocated that love, and together they cherished Eric.

Eric's third birthday could not have come quick enough for the family. In June 1986, the Morton's went to Houston for the surgery and came home two weeks later with a healthy son. He was full of energy rather than tired and depleted for the first time. The family came home with a healthy son and a fresh outlook. Maybe the weight that had been so heavy on their shoulders could diminish and make room for newfound love in their lives.

Even with the loss of their first child, Michael described his family as 'almost excruciatingly average. We were a chunk out of a demographic study. The house, the yard, the kid, the car. We had everything but the picket fence. It was good.' It seems reminiscent of the American dream, but what's our understanding of it now? Often, those dreams can swiftly morph into nightmares.

On 13 August 1986, Michael rose quietly from his sheets at dawn, trying his best not to disturb Christine. They had celebrated Michael's 32nd Birthday the night before. He had a day off from work and decided to spend it doing one of his favourite activities. Scuba diving in nearby Lake Travis. After scuba diving, Michael went home and took a nap to prepare to celebrate with his family in the evening.

It was a fun evening at first. They brought Eric to the City Grill, a trendy restaurant in downtown Austin, for a rare night out.

They smiled at their son, now the epitome of health, digging into a bowl of ice cream. Eric nodded off in the car on the way home, and when they arrived, Michael carried him to his room and tucked him in.

Once he and Christine were alone, to Michael, it was the perfect opportunity; it was his birthday, their child was happily sound asleep, and he wanted to get lucky. Michael put on an adult film he had rented for the occasion, hoping to spark some romance.

They curled up on the blanket on the floor in front of the fireplace. Michael poured in some wine, about to make a move, but Eric came running down the hallway.

Christine got up to put Eric back to bed and then returned to the blanket on the floor. Michael tried again, but Christine was exhausted, and she fell asleep. Hurt and angry, Michael retreated to the bedroom without her. Later, she leaned over and kissed him when she came to bed. Tomorrow night, she promised.

The episode had left Michael feeling out of sorts and rankled. Michael left a note for Christine on the bathroom vanity the next morning. The note said:

'Chris, I know you didn't mean to, but you made me feel unwanted last night. With your nightgown around your waist and while I was rubbing your hands and arms, fell asleep. [...] Just think how you might have felt if you were left hanging on your birthday.'

He ended the note by scribbling, 'I L Y' I love you and signed it 'M.'

No matter the duration of your marriage or relationship, there's no implicit agreement to engage in sex whenever your partner desires it. Consent works both ways; if you're uncomfortable, you're entitled to say no without explanation. You shouldn't feel obligated to justify your choice. Even having a ribbing relationship has its limits and its line, and that note runs that line over like a stampede.

Admittedly, couples often have heated moments they regret later. Yet, I find it hard to believe that Michael wrote this note expecting it to eventually be used as incriminating evidence against him.

After leaving the note, Michael left for work at 5.30 am as he always did. In the early afternoon hours, Morton's neighbour, Elizabeth Gee, was working in the yard when she saw Eric sitting on the front steps of the Morton house.

Eric kept going in and out of the house and often peeked around the car in the Morton driveway to look at Elizabeth. At around noon, Elizabeth realised she hadn't seen Christine with Eric, so she picked Eric up. Noticing that his diaper was heavy and needed to be changed, she walked into the Morton's house and called for Christine. But she couldn't find her. So, she took Eric back to her place so he could play with her son.

Elizabeth returned a bit later, hoping she had turned up by now. In the Morton's bedroom, Elizabeth saw some dresser drawers dumped on the floor and covers pulled around the bed.

Tucked in at the top where a pillow should be, Elizabeth saw a pile of blankets and a blue suitcase. This was strange. Then, she saw the wall and ceiling were splattered with blood. Elizabeth lifted the covers and found Christine's wrist.

She felt for a pulse.

But found nothing. She ran back to her house and called the police.

Michael followed his routine that day, heading to work and clocking in at 6.05 am. He spent the morning chatting with Mario Garcia, the produce manager, sharing their passion for scuba diving and even making plans for an upcoming dive. However, everything turned unexpectedly when he returned home from Redden's. He was met with a startling sight: crime scene tape cordoning off his residence, a swarm of police officers, and curious neighbours braving the oppressive heat, seeking a glimpse of the unfolding events.

When Michael reached his house, his heart pounding, he headed for the door. But before he could enter, Sheriff Boutwell intercepted him, inquiring about his identity.

To those unfamiliar, Sheriff Jim Boutwell of Williamson County embodied a stereotype: a deliberate speaker, a former Texas Ranger sporting a white Stetson, and a black coffee enthusiast. He exuded an air of authority, having once calmly disarmed a potentially volatile situation by calmly dispossessing a man holding a gun.

Boutwell, however, operated according to his own standards, leading to a mishandled case. In 1983, three years before Christine's tragic death, Boutwell extracted a confession from Henry Lee Lucas, a one-eyed wanderer who would later be labelled the most prolific serial killer in American history within a short span. Invited by the Montague sheriff to probe Lucas regarding the unsolved Orange Socks murder case in Williamson County, Boutwell engaged in an initially promising investigation. He brought Lucas back, coaxing further details about the killing, but his methods were morally dubious. Boutwell fed Lucas information, recording his confession multiple times for refinement.

In 1983, Boutwell and a team of officers coerced hundreds of murder confessions from Lucas. He was provided with crime-scene photos and details about alleged victims, offered comforts like milkshakes and access to a colour TV, and assured that he wouldn't face death row if he kept talking. Consequently, Lucas provided investigators with graphic specifics, leading to his indictment for 189 homicides. However, none of his claims were supported by fingerprints, weapons, or eyewitnesses. Subsequently sentenced to death, an Attorney General's report by Jim Mattox discredited many of Lucas's confessions, revealing that he wasn't even in the same state during some of the purported killings.

Michael responded before inquiring about Eric's well-being. Boutwell confirmed Eric's safety, mentioning he was at his neighbour's house. Subsequently, Michael asked about Christine, and Boutwell delivered the stark news that Christine had died.

In his memoir, Michael expressed feeling suffocated, as if he were engulfed in water. Despite this, on the day in question, he appeared disoriented. There was no visible response to the news of Christine's passing. It's crucial to acknowledge that individuals express grief and sorrow uniquely.

Subsequently, he was ushered inside the house for a conversation. Boutwell ensured Michael was informed of his Miranda rights, after which Sergeant Don Wood, the lead investigator, requested Michael's signature on a consent form authorizing the police to search his residence and vehicle.

Boutwell and Wood spent the next few hours questioning Michael about his life, marriage, and what he had done that day. Michael, who did not request an attorney, was cooperative and candid during his conversation with Boutwell and Wood. He depicted his day in painstaking detail, down to what colour of socks he had worn to bed. Soon, questions drifted to that of tensions in his marriage whether either of them had had an affair. Sensing the fatalistic turn in the conversation, Michael said at one point he didn't do it, whatever it is.

At this point, he had just received news that had destroyed his viewpoint of the world. He's dazed and trying to muddle through. And guess what got brought up? The note Michael had left in the bathroom.

Michael admitted he wrote it; he confirmed he wished he hadn't.

Sheriff's deputies brushed past him, opening drawers and rifling through cabinets. He could see the light of a camera flash exploding again and again in the master bedroom as a police photographer documented what Michael realized must have been the place where Christine was killed. People were rifling through his life and home, and he witnessed it like he was detached.

The police asked if Michael noticed anything important missing from the house, and he realised that the 45-calibre pistol he kept on the top shelf of their closet was missing.

Following extensive interrogation, Michael finally had the chance to reunite with his son. Boutwell, Wood, and Michael proceeded to the neighbour's residence, where they found Eric. The child appeared unkempt and visibly distressed, showing signs of having cried extensively. This young boy probably witnessed his mother's tragic demise.

Michael and Eric eventually made their way back to the Morton house. Michael insisted on staying in the home because he could still feel Christine. As if they could be with her for just a little longer. Some would remark that it is a bit strange that he returned to the house, considering it was a crime scene. Furniture was overturned, clothes were strewn across the floor, and the kitchen was littered with empty Coke cans and cigarette butts courtesy of the investigators. But Michael's main priority was his son.

He spent the evening trying to create a semblance of normalcy for Eric. Eric ate, and they played until it was time for bed. After falling asleep, Michael eventually went to his and Christine's bedroom. When he turned on the light, he saw blood on the ceiling and on the headboard.

He spent the rest of the night lying next to Eric or pacing the house. By morning, he was joined by both his and Christine's family. Michael was concerned primarily with Eric's well-being, so he arranged for Eric to meet with a child therapist so that a professional could assess his mental health and the effects of his mother's murder. He was relieved when the therapist told him that his son was experiencing no more than the usual signs and manifestations of separation anxiety that often followed the death of a parent. But there was no indication that he had been victimised. It is good to note that Wood had already tried to question the boy but could not get any information from him.

The day following Christine's murder, her brother John searched the Morton house and property. He found a bloodstained blue bandana about a hundred yards behind the Morton household, adjacent to the woods. John gave the bandana to detectives, and it was found that the bandana had blood and a single hair on it. But, due to the limitations of DNA testing at the time, it was impossible to tell if the blood was Christine's or not.

But it couldn't be matched to Michael either.

It is also on this day that the police willfully ignore a new lead.

Orin Holland, who lived one block north of the Mortons on Adonis Drive, stopped a sheriff's deputy who was canvassing the neighbourhood to share what he thought might be important information. Holland told the officer that on several occasions, his wife, Mary and a neighbour; Joni St Martin, had seen a man park a green van by the vacant, wooded lot behind the Morton home. They had also seen the man get out of the van and walk into the overgrown area that extended up to the Morton's privacy fence.

Orin kept waiting for the police to come and talk to them or ask them more questions, but to their surprise, they never did.

When looking for more substantial evidence, investigators found fingerprints on the sliding glass door that did not match anyone in the Morton household. So, not Michael.

Another fingerprint, also unidentified, was lifted from the blue suitcase that had been stacked on top of Christine's body. The police also found a fresh footprint inside Morton's fenced backyard.

The subsequent step would involve examining Christine's autopsy performed by Dr. Robert Bayardo. As per Bayardo's findings, she sustained a minimum of eight blows to her head. Bayardo's assessment suggests that Christine likely succumbed before the third strike. The assault occurred while she was asleep, indicating that she might not have had ample time to comprehend the situation or endure prolonged suffering.

There was a six-inch long, two-and-a-half-inch wide cut through her forehead. Her nose and upper jaw were fractured, and her face was so beaten that the pathologist could not determine the colour of her eyes. He found long, jagged splinters of wood embedded in her head. He also determined that Christine had not been sexually assaulted. So, that rules out two motives, but the savagery of the beating itself seemed to suggest that rage was a contributing factor.

Based on an analysis of partially digested food found in Christine's stomach, the medical examiner had estimated that she had been killed between one and six o'clock in the morning (Michael had, by his own account, been at home with her until five-thirty). The results did not necessarily implicate Michael but did not clear him of suspicion.

Michael was summoned to the police station for further interrogation. Despite having already provided information, he endured hours of repetitive questioning. Michael requested a polygraph test to vindicate himself, an idea that intrigued Boutwell. They arranged the polygraph for that evening at the Department of Public Safety (DPS). Although Michael arrived punctually, after enduring extensive delays, he requested to postpone. Understandably, this reflected poorly on Michael's position, leaving Boutwell dissatisfied.

Time started to crawl on for Eric and Michael, who bid his mother to go home after she had been there to support the two through this ideal. That night, Michael cooked dinner for himself and Eric, and they were having a good night. Michael described that evening as the first time he had felt at home in a long time. They even danced in the kitchen. But as he was cooking dinner, Michael heard a knock on the door. Sheriff Boutwell, Sergeant Wood, and a few other officers were there to arrest Michael.

From the start, Boutwell treated Michael not like a grieving husband but like a suspect. And the circumstances did not help Michael's case in the slightest. His opinion of Michael was influenced by the note left in the bathroom for Christine, establishing that he was angry with her in the hours leading up to the murder. Michael's lack of emotion at the news of her death did not do much to dispel the suspicion that this was a domestic affair. Moreover, there were no indications of a break-in. In fact, the sliding glass door in the dining area was unlocked. Robbery did not appear to have been a motive for the crime because whilst Christine's purse was missing, her engagement ring and wedding band were lying in plain sight on the nightstand.

Michael was informed that some neighbours had arranged to take care of Eric until Michael's parents could get into town. Still, the officers could have easily contacted Michael about his impending arrest and allowed him to turn himself in while planning for his son's care. Instead, they made it a spectacle, making Eric watch, screaming as his dad was taken away from him.

Michael's bond was around $250,000, which he couldn't pay. So, he stayed in jail for a week until he was granted a bond reduction. After being released on bond, Michael was met with the witch-hunt of being accused of his wife's murder. Sheriff Boutwell did not let up, and they intentionally sullied Michael's name around the town, giving fragments of information to the media, even reporting that there was no sign of a break-in, adding to the suspicion surrounding Michael.

Boutwell also told reporters that there was not an indication of robbery at the scene despite the apparent disarray, conveniently missing anything about Christine's missing purse or gun. These misdemeanours could taint a prospective jury pool.

But as we already know, this isn't the first time the sheriff has played by his own rules. Our sheriff seems fixed on his idea of justice, unwilling to consider alternative perspectives. This doesn't bode well for Michael's situation. This sheriff was focusing on his tunnel vision despite its many dangers.

As reported by Texas Monthly, weeks after the funeral, Eric uttered words that left Michael stunned. Michael was meticulously cleaning the bathtub in the master bathroom when Eric approached from behind. The child's gaze fixated on the shower, scrutinizing it, and he asked if his dad knew who the man who was in the shower with his clothes on.

Michael sat back, stunned. He had no doubt that Eric was speaking of the man who had killed Christine. The boy's question dovetailed with details from the crime scene; there had been blood on the bathroom door. Hesitant to say anything that might upset his son, Michael did not probe further. Instead, he encouraged him to speak to his therapist.

His therapist would never glean any further details from Eric, and Michael did not disclose the boy's statement to the Sheriff's Office. Given how aggressively Boutwell and Wood had questioned him, Michael did not want them near his son.

Sergeant Wood even showed up at a local Neighbourhood Watch meeting and told attendees present that he had suspicions about Michael, then he even asked people to raise their hands if they thought Michael killed Christine.

Boutwell made sure the community believed that Michael was a sex-driven maniac who beat his wife to death because she wouldn't have sex on his birthday. Michael's neighbours treated him like he was guilty, friends ignored him, people whispered. He was already in a prison of someone else's making. Other co-workers welcomed him back in the blink of an eye, like Mario Garcia. Garcia, who had let Michael into the Safeway on the day Christine was murdered, had always been certain that he was innocent. Mario confirmed to Texas Monthly he never doubted Michael because of Eric. After everything he did to make Eric well, why would he leave him at a crime scene?

In the five months leading to his trial for the murder of his wife, Michael continued to work forty hours a week at Safeway, as he couldn't be fired unless he was convicted of a crime, and he parented Eric as well as he could. But the notoriety of the crime plagued him wherever he went. Customers approached him, asking if the person who killed his wife worked there.

In the months preceding the trial, sheriff's deputies frequently visited the Gee residence to talk to Elizabeth, who was still grappling with the trauma of finding Christine's body. However, rather than providing solace, these visits were distressing. As per Christopher, Elizabeth's husband at the time, the deputies would plant notions about Michael engaging in drug dealing, instilling fear by suggesting she needed to exercise caution due to uncertainty about Michael's potential actions.

Elizabeth's testimony stood as a pivotal element for the prosecution. Not only did she stumble upon Christine's body, but she also overheard Michael's less compassionate remarks about her. Despite the pressure from sheriff deputies, her account promised value for the prosecution's case. Michael's perceived emotional detachment regarding Christine's death only compounded the situation.

Adding to the complexity and further implicating Michael, the Travis County medical examiner, Roberto Bayardo, who had conducted Christine's autopsy, modified the estimated time of her death. Notably, Bayardo previously collaborated with Boutwell on the Orange Socks case. Initially, based on his assumption that she dined as late as 11.00 pm, Bayardo's findings suggested Christine could have passed away as late as 6.00 am, merely thirty minutes after Michael had left for work. However, during later testimony, the medical examiner admitted to determining this without all the pertinent facts, notably lacking information about Christine's final meal.

Bayardo altered his assessment soon after Boutwell and Anderson's trip to the City Grill, obtaining a credit card receipt indicating Michael's payment for their meal at 9.21 pm. With Bayardo's updated time of death, it became implausible for Christine to have died after 1.30 am. Absent this revelation, there was scant evidence against Michael.

On 10 February 1987, the case of The State of Texas v Michael W. Morton commenced. Michael had not made any arrangements for Eric's care in case he was convicted. He was cautiously optimistic that he would not be found guilty.

Securing an unbiased jury was a formidable challenge due to the sheriff's influence on public opinion against Michael, compounded by the widespread awareness of Christine's murder. Eventually, the prosecution and defence assembled a jury comprising seven individuals. The prosecution's case, based on circumstantial evidence, alleged that Michael fatally assaulted Christine because she refused to engage in sexual activity on his 32nd birthday. They posited that he staged a burglary afterwards to conceal his actions.

The defence said that Christine was alive and asleep in bed when Michael left for work at around 5.30 am. Then, an intruder killed Christine after Michael left for work, stole Michael's gun and Christine's purse and wallet, then fled to the woods behind the Morton household. Suppose we were to use Occam's Razor without looking at the evidence and the circumstances. In that case, it seems more likely that Michael would murder her, but now that we know Michael's story and the intervention of the sheriff and prosecution, the idea that Michael did it is dubious.

In the absence of any concrete evidence, the prosecutors relied on emotional material, such as Elizabeth Gee, who painted a portrait of an unhappy marriage, and how aloof Michael had been in the weeks that followed Christine's death. Her disgust for Michael was palpable, leading the jury to dislike him.

Building on the idea that Michael hated his wife, the prosecution also cast him as sexually deviant. Over the protests of the defence, Judge Lott allowed the district attorney to show jurors the first two minutes of Handful of Diamonds, the adult video that Michael had rented, under the pretext that it established his state of mind before the murder. The jury was less than impressed with the content. They thought Michael was a sadist. He was seen as callous and unrepentant and no doubt capable of murder.

The prosecution then called Bayardo to the stand to provide testimony that would, in effect, place Michael at the scene of the crime. Bayardo told the jury that Christine had died within four hours of eating her last meal. However, he added that his estimated time of death was an opinion based on his experience and not a scientific statement (When Bayardo was asked in 2011 to clarify what he had meant by this, he said under oath that his estimate was not based on real science.)

The defence team, Allison and White, mounted a vigorous defence, calling expert witnesses who cast severe doubts on Bayardo's time of death estimate. But they did not have a cohesive story to tell. If Michael didn't kill Christine, they still didn't know who did. He and White wove together the facts they had in their arsenal – the unidentified fingerprints, the unlocked glass door, the footprint in the backyard. But there was a catch: Sergeant Wood was never called to testify, and if he was never called to testify, neither did his notes.

Without access to his notes, they could not present the whole picture; they did not know about the reports of a mysterious green van behind the Morton home, and they failed to understand the importance of the discarded bandana with a blood stain. Allison and White didn't mention the man Eric saw either; the chances that the judge would allow a three-year-old to testify were slim to none, and Michael would probably object.

Michael composedly testified, addressing questions with unwavering steadiness despite the tragic loss of his wife and the upheaval of his life. He aimed to project strength, yet ironically, this resolute demeanour worked against him as jurors were unsettled by his fortitude.

As the guilty verdict was read, Michael's legs went weak, and he had to be supported by one of his attorneys. Finally, he fell back into his chair, rested his head on the defence table, and wept. He insisted before he was sentenced to life in prison, pleading to the judge, pleading that he didn't do it.[4]

During his twenty-five years in prison, Michael was sure he would be vindicated, and he kept himself busy as his attorneys worked on his appeals. He majored in psychology at Sam Houston University and eventually obtained his Bachelor's degree.

In his memoir, Michael depicted prison as dehumanising; he was to scrape drainage ditches and perform backbreaking labour so he could work towards his degree. He recalled looking into a room and getting a cup of urine thrown in his face. Prison is all about routine, followed by routine and then more routine.

In the midst of losing his life, he was also in the midst of losing his son. Christine's family filed for custody of Eric, resulting in a nasty custody battle between Christine and his own family. Especially since Boutwell had convinced Christine's family that Michael had killed her, Christine's family won custody of Eric, who went to live with Christine's sister, Marylee. The court ordered that Marylee allow Eric to see Michael every six months until he was eighteen.

The poor boy did not even recognise his father. He was a new child every time he visited, and Michael didn't get to watch him grow. To Michael's despair, when Eric was 15, he wrote his dad a letter saying he did not want to visit someone he barely knew anymore. Eric was all he had left, and he was gone.

While Michael was incarcerated, there were multiple appeals to reopen his case, especially with DNA technology rising in fame. In July 2002, fifteen years after his conviction, Michael discovered that the Innocence Project was taking on his case.

Almost three years later, in 2005, Michael's attorneys filed requests for testing on multiple items found at the crime scene. The items included the bandana, fingernail scrapings from Christine and evidence from an unsolved murder eerily similar to Christine's.

In January 1988, two years following Christine's tragic murder, Deborah Masters Bake suffered a similar fate, being fatally beaten in her Austin residence. Disturbingly, there were striking parallels between the murders of Christine and Deborah. Both women had long, dark hair, were mothers to young children, and were fatally assaulted in their sleep by unidentified blunt-force trauma to the head.

However, the crucial disparity lies in the fact that while Christine's case led to a conviction, Deborah's murder remained unsolved, leaving the perpetrator unidentified and justice elusive.

The court granted testing on some items, including the fingernail scrapings, but denied testing the bandana and the evidence collected from Deborah's murder. Regrettably, the test results from the permitted testing could not exclude Michael as the murderer.

In October 2008, Texas Attorney General Greg Abbott ordered Williamson County District Attorney John Bradley to give Michael's lawyers the investigative documents regarding Christine's murder.

This is where Michael's attorneys found their treasure trove. They found the plethora of evidence Sergeant Wood had never turned over to the defence, including the accounts of the Morton's neighbours who witnessed the man parking and exiting a van behind the Morton home before walking towards their backyard fence.

The day after Christine was murdered, a San Antonio business, the Jewel Box, contacted the Williamson County Sheriff's Office to report that someone had left Christine's credit card in the store. Whoever took the call wrote a note to Sergeant Wood, but it is unclear if it was followed up.

The notes also discussed the man Eric saw. Still, Wood believed that Eric was simply mistaken and theorised that Michael had been wearing a full-body scuba diving suit at the time of Christine's murder, which is why Eric didn't recognise his own father.

It wasn't until January 2010, twenty-three years after Michael had been convicted of his wife's murder, that the Third Court of Appeals in Austin allowed the bandana to be tested for DNA. The DNA test results showed that a hair and some blood on the bandana was from Christine. There was also the presence of a single unidentified DNA profile from a man.

The man was not Michael Morton.

On 19 August 2011, the DNA was put into CODIS, a national database and a match was made. The DNA was from a man named Mark Allen Norwood.

Mark had felony convictions from at least four states, including arrests in Texas, California and Tennessee for aggravated assault with intent to kill, arson, breaking and entering residences, drug possession and resisting arrest. To top it off, Mark lived less than a mile away from the victim of a similar murder, Deborah Master Baker, at the time of her murder.

Almost twenty-five years to the day after Christine was murdered, Michael was called by and told that the man whose DNA was found on the bandana had been identified. Silence was on the other line until Michael said he was letting the news wash all over him.

As dramatic as the DNA results were, the Williamson County district attorney's office was not ready to admit that Michael had been wrongly convicted.

Innocence Project lawyer Nina Morrison and Houston lawyer John Rayleigh sat down with the Austin Police Department cold case team. The lawyers handed over the information they had on Mark Horwood.

After reviewing the new information, police investigated him further, and a hair was found at the scene of Deborah's murder matching his DNA.

Two days later, Judge Billy Ray Stubblefield ordered Wood's reports regarding Christine's murder to be unsealed. Michael's lawyers found that Judge Lott was not given all the reports he requested in the days leading up to Michael's trial.

In fact, all that was given were two documents: a five-page supplementary offence report/results of investigation prepared on the day Christine was found dead and a one-page form from Michael saying his house could be searched.

It is concerning that Lott only believed that two documents could have been accumulated from a nine-month-long investigation. The tunnel vision was imminent when he accepted these short documents as the only evidence and had them sealed.

On 26 September 2011, Michael's attorneys argued that they needed to be released as soon as possible, but the Williamson County prosecutors wanted more time to review the evidence, just to rub more salt in the wound.

Four days later, the Williamson County District Attorney contacted Michael's attorneys and said they needed to discuss freeing Michael. The DA agreed that Michael would never have been convicted if the jury had all the information and that Michael should immediately be released.

And he was.

On 4 October 2011, Michael Morton was released from prison. He had been incarcerated for twenty-four years, seven months and eleven days. A total of 8995 days of his life had been taken from him; he had lost his wife and his son.

After his release, Michal moved in with his parents in Liberty City, Texas.

Although he was thankful for his freedom, he recalled in his memoir how he had a lot of learning to do.

Many things had changed over the last twenty-five years, just having a mobile phone blew his mind.

A few weeks after his release, Michael met with Eric, now a grown man, with a wife and expecting their own child. Initially struggling with reconciliation, it was challenging to meet with Michael, especially after being raised by Christine's sister and family, alongside the lies surrounding his father.

Michael found out that Eric didn't know much about Christine; it was so hard for her family to talk about her that they rarely did. Therefore, Michael made it his goal to tell Eric about his mother and celebrate her.

On 9 December 2011, a few weeks later, Mark Norwood was arrested and charged with the capital murder of Christine Morton. Michael was officially exonerated.[5]

On 16 November 2011, Morton's original prosecutor, Ken Anderson, told reporters: 'I want to formally apologize for the system's failure to Mr. Morton. In hindsight, the verdict was wrong.'[6] Since Michael's trial, Ken Anderson had become a state district judge.

Anderson faced a tribunal regarding his conduct during the investigation, with debates arising over allegations of tampering and withholding evidence. He was charged with criminal contempt, leading to his resignation as a state district judge and voluntary surrender of his law license. His sentence of ten days in jail was reduced due to good behaviour, resulting in a serving time of only ninety-six hours.

Sheriff Jim Boutwell died in 1993 and obviously could not be made to respond to his own actions in the case.

Despite how he was treated, Michael harbours no animosity toward law enforcement – they're the good guys, he says – but warns anyone who will listen to get legal representation the moment they're fingered.

On 16 May 2013, Governor of Texas Rick Perry signed Texas Senate Bill 1611, also called the Michael Morton Act, into law. The Act is designed to ensure a more open discovery process. The bill's open file policy removes barriers to accessing evidence. Morton was present to sign the bill, which became law on 1 September 2013.[7]

After his decades-long fight for freedom, Michael married Cynthia May Chessman, a woman he met at church after his release from prison.

When the couple married, they asked their two hundred guests to donate to the Innocence Project instead of giving them gifts.

He is also a grandfather to Eric and his wife Maggie's daughter. She has her late grandmother's bright eyes, and her name is Christine.

Michael Morton was the victim of severe prosecutorial misconduct that caused him to lose twenty-five years of his life and completely ripped apart from his family. Perhaps even more tragically, we now know that another murder might have been prevented. Norwood could have been found and convicted if law enforcement had continued its investigation rather than building a false case against Michael. While the investigators went off unfortunate statistics and circumstantial evidence, such as Michael's approach and less than favourable relationship with Christine, they wilfully ignored physical evidence. It shows how blinding tunnel vision can really be. Occam's Razor should have been used as a rule of thumb to narrow down what could have happened to Christine. Instead, the most simplistic theory was looked at and run without consideration of the emotional impact it would have on Michael and his family. They were negligent, an example of how the criminal justice system still has flaws.

Conclusion

Are There Limitations With
Simplicity Within True Crime?

I t is often hard to write a conclusion. This book is a sum of its parts, but what collective significance do these parts hold? What questions can they answer, or what questions do they spark? The exploration of these true crime cases aimed to spotlight them and to ascertain if they address this fundamental question: 'Are there limitations with simplicity within true crime?' Does a heuristic rule of thumb such as Occam's Razor pose limits or offer remedies? Should its influence be as substantial as it is often granted?

Are there limitations to simplicity within true crime? Absolutely. Simplification might ignore essential contextual factors that contribute to the crime. Socioeconomic, psychological, and historical backgrounds can significantly influence criminal behaviour, and oversimplification might disregard these crucial aspects. Over-emphasizing simplicity might lead investigators or the audience to favour one straightforward explanation while ignoring other plausible hypotheses. This could prevent a thorough examination of all possible angles of a case. Criminal behaviour is inherently multifaceted, shaped by emotions, psychology, and societal influences. Simplifying such behaviour might not accurately represent the complexity of human actions and motivations.

While simplicity can offer clarity, it's crucial to balance simplicity with a comprehensive understanding of the complexities involved in true crime. Investigating and interpreting these cases often necessitates a nuanced approach considering multiple perspectives and factors. This is where Occam's Razor should come into play.

We understand that Occam's Razor, coined after William of Ockham, means the simplest answer is the best starting point to investigate and that entities should not be multiplied beyond necessity. Occam's Razor can sometimes be misinterpreted as the simplest explanation is always right, which leads to problematic simplification bias, often dismissing complex but accurate explanations in favour of simpler, incomplete ones.

Sometimes, the simplest explanation is the correct one. Sometimes, there are the usual suspects. Look at the case of Jerika Binks; when everyone was out looking for a culprit, they didn't think the weather conditions and the terrain got the better of her. However, with Dana Laskowski, it wasn't any previous romantic interest that may have gotten jealous and attacked her; it was her niece's best friend.

Occam's Razor can be useful within the realms of true crime to help investigators wade through the quagmire of theories and suspects. It can be used in the early stages of an investigation to encourage starting with simpler explanations before exploring more complex and convoluted possibilities. It can help in organizing the investigation process efficiently. If that had been done with the case of Jacob Wetterling, there is a chance that his murder could have been resolved sooner.

Nevertheless, Occam's Razor is a double-edged sword. Relying solely on Occam's Razor can lead to biases or tunnel vision, where investigators might favour simple explanations that align with their preconceptions, overlooking alternative, more accurate theories. Michael Morton might not have lost years of his life and the opportunity to watch his son grow up if Occam's Razor hadn't been solely depended on.

Occam's Razor can be used as a guideline but not an absolute. People always forget the beginning of the razor. In testing multiple hypotheses, test the one with the fewest parts first. It's not 'the simplest solution is probably true'. That's just false. A non-sequitur. The razor is a practical rule of thumb about applying the scientific method, not a resounding statement of probability.

We must never forget that people are full of multitudes. While Occam's Razor can avoid overcomplication and allow investigators to prioritize essential evidence and factors while avoiding unnecessary assumptions and complexities, criminal cases often involve multifaceted motives, actions, and circumstances. Often, intricate details, contexts and behaviour nuances need to be examined. Over-reliance on simplicity might disregard these crucial aspects necessary for a comprehensive understanding of a crime.

As much as we might crave an explanation for closure and tidiness, that analysis is often too clinical, and the world does not work with that much precision. Police officers, investigators, and *we* must understand that cases are often complex whilst considering the existence of prior statistics to help recognise patterns. Statistics are valuable, but they are just one piece of the puzzle; they should be used alongside other investigative techniques.

Regardless, we can take from this that the culture of policing gets in the way of solving crimes due to the hindrance of information sharing, the Us vs Them Mentality, exemplified in the case of Jane Britton. Some police cultures foster an 'us vs. them' mentality, where there's a perceived division between law enforcement and the community.

This can hinder cooperation and information sharing with the public, affecting the flow of critical information needed to solve crimes. Policing cultures can be influenced by biases or stereotypes, impacting how investigations are conducted. This might lead to certain cases being prioritized over others based on biases or suspects being treated differently based on preconceived notions. There is also a lack of accountability, as proved by Jim Boutwell and his methods of cohesion.

While acknowledging these negative impacts, instances like Ken Brennan's comprehensive investigation into Greg Fleniken's murder highlight positive contributions.

A conclusion or concluding chapter implies the conversation and analysis have come to a close and we have our answers. However, with true crime, the conversation is never over. We need to make sure we are doing everything in our power to make sure survivors have voices, to make sure families get the closure they need, and the trauma they go through is not glamorised. It is vital to remember the people who never backed down and never gave up on looking for answers for their loved ones.

It is easy for me to write a book about true crime and for readers such as yourselves to consume it; however, it is vital that the conversation surrounding true crime itself is not glamourized and is respectful. At the end of the day, these aren't fictional characters within these pages; they are people living with the fact that their lives have been changed.

We need to approach these tragedies with empathy and sensitivity, use the knowledge gained from these stories to raise awareness about safety precautions and provide resources available for those affected by similar situations. We must support organizations or initiatives towards crime prevention and victim support. We need to discuss those who might not be presented by the media and ensure their voices are heard.

It is imperative to remember the names: Dana Laskowski, Jane Britton, Juliana Redding, Jacob Wetterling, Greg Fleniken, Jerika Binks, Gareth Williams, Mike Williams, The McStay Family and Michael Morton.

The world itself is multifaceted, messy and complicated. There are so many stories that are yet to be heard. All we need to do is listen.

Notes

Introduction

1. Serena, K. (2021) *Diane Schuler was the perfect PTA Mom, so why did she kill 8 people with her van?, All That's Interesting.* Available at: https://allthatsinteresting.com/diane-schuler (Accessed: November 26, 2022).

2. *Wrong way tragedy: Supporting first responders* (2015) *Rivertowns Daily Voice.* Available at: https://dailyvoice.com/new-york/rivertowns/news/wrong-way-tragedy-supporting-first-responders/430461/ (Accessed: November 26, 2022).

3. Stuever, H. (2011) *TV review: 'there's something wrong with Aunt Diane', The Washington Post.* WP Company. Available at: https://www.washingtonpost.com/lifestyle/style/tv-review-theres-something-wrong-with-aunt-diane/2011/07/20/gIQARBkCXI_story.html (Accessed: November 26, 2022).

4. James, S.D. (2010) *Husband of Taconic Crash's Diane Schuler Sues N.Y. State, ABC News.* ABC News Network. Available at: https://abcnews.go.com/Health/taconic-crashes-diane-schuler-super-mom-perfectionist-hbo/story?id=14152213 (Accessed: November 26, 2022).

5. *Settlements reached in 4 Taconic Parkway wrong-way crash lawsuits* (2014) *CBS News.* Available at: https://www.cbsnews.com/newyork/news/settlements-reached-in-4-taconic-parkway-wrong-way-crash-lawsuits/ (Accessed: 21 August 2023).

6. *Occam's Razor definition & meaning* (no date) *Merriam-Webster.* Merriam-Webster. Available at: https://www.merriam-webster.com/dictionary/Occam%27s%20razor (Accessed: November 26, 2022).

7. *https://www.merriam-webster.com/dictionary/parsimony* (no date) *Merriam Webster.* Available at: https://www.merriam-webster.com/dictionary/parsimony.

8. Partington, V. (2021) *Killer hitchhiker: The murder of Dorothy Donovan, Medium.* Medium. Available at: https://veritycreates.medium.com/killer-hitchhiker-the-murder-of-dorothy-donovan-b6c5dfc6d359 (Accessed: November 26, 2022).

9. Pundir, R. (2022) *Solved mysteries that seem strange even for us, Ranker.* Ranker. Available at: https://www.ranker.com/list/strange-solved-mysteries/rima-pundir (Accessed: November 26, 2022).

10. Farnam Street (2019) *How to use Occam's Razor without getting cut, Farnam Street.* Available at: https://fs.blog/occams-razor/ (Accessed: 21 August 2023).

Chapter One

1. *https://www.imdb.com/title/tt0118884/* (no date) *IMDB.* Available at: https://www.imdb.com/title/tt0118884/.

2. "Ockham's razor". *Encyclopædia Britannica.* Encyclopædia Britannica Online. 2010. Archived from the original on 23 August 2010. Retrieved 12 June 2010.

3. *Summa Totius Logicae*, i. 12, cited in "Ockham's Razor" by Paul Newall at *Galilean Library* (25 June 2005)

4. *Mental shortcuts* (no date) *National Geographic Society*. Available at: https://education.nationalgeographic.org/resource/mental-shortcuts (Accessed: November 27, 2022).

5. Cherry, K. (2022) *What is cognitive bias?*, *Verywell Mind*. Verywell Mind. Available at: https://www.verywellmind.com/what-is-a-cognitive-bias-2794963 (Accessed: November 30, 2022).

6. 'Lisa's Pony' (1991) The Simpsons, series three, episode eight. Directed by Carlos Baeza. Written by Matt Groening

Chapter Two

1. Bumbrah, G.S. (2017) "Cyanoacrylate fuming method for detection of Latent Fingermarks: A Review," *Egyptian Journal of Forensic Sciences*, 7(1). Available at: https://doi.org/10.1186/s41935-017-0009-7.

2. Stockton, C. (2021) *The murderer who wrote 'kill someone + get away with it' on her bucket list*, *Thought Catalog*. Available at: https://thoughtcatalog.com/christine-stockton/2021/04/the-murderer-who-wrote-kill-someone-get-away-with-it-on-her-bucket-list/ (Accessed: December 28, 2022).

3. Vanapalli, V. (2021) *Dana Laskowski murder: Where is Emily Lauenborg now?*, *The Cinemaholic*. Available at: https://thecinemaholic.com/dana-laskowski-murder-where-is-emily-lauenborg-now/ (Accessed: December 28, 2022).

Chapter Three

1. Vonnegut, K. (2007). *The Sirens of Titan*. Dial Press.

2. *Music student at B.U. throttled by strangler in apt. Near Square: News: The Harvard Crimson* (1963) *News | The Harvard Crimson*. Available at: https://www.thecrimson.com/article/1963/5/9/music-student-at-bu-throttled-by/ (Accessed: 09 September 2023).

3. Reinhold, Robert (January 18, 1969). "Cambridge Murder Victim Is Recalled as Intelligent and Witty". The New York Times. Retrieved December 29, 2018. Available at https://timesmachine.nytimes.com/timesmachine/1969/01/19/90039924.html?action=click&contentCollection=Archives&module=ArticleEndCTA&region=ArchiveBody&pgtype=article&pageNumber=62

4. de Saint Phalle, Anne (January 8, 1969). "Grad Student Killed". *The Harvard Crimson*. Retrieved December 30, 2018.

5. "Services Held for Slain Coed". *Associated Press*. January 9, 1969. Retrieved December 30, 2018 – via Lewiston Evening Journal.

6. "Cambridge Police Declare Black-out On Britton Case". *The Harvard Crimson*. January 10, 1969. Retrieved December 31, 2022. Available at https://www.thecrimson.com/article/1969/1/10/cambridge-police-declare-black-out-on-britton/

7. *We keep the dead close: A murder at Harvard and a Half Century of silence by Becky Cooper* (2020) *Goodreads*. Goodreads. Available at: https://www.goodreads.com/book/show/52041387-we-keep-the-dead-close (Accessed: January 15, 2023).

8. MacNeill, Arianna (November 20, 2018). "Jane Britton, a Harvard graduate student, was found murdered in 1969. Now authorities say they know who did it". *Boston.com*. Retrieved January 2, 2019.

9. "DNA Used to Identify Man Responsible for 1969 Murder of Jane Britton" (PDF) (Press release). Woburn, Massachusetts: Middlesex County District Attorney's Office. Retrieved December 30, 2022. Available at https://www.middlesexda.com/sites/middlesexda/files/news/press_packet_-_jane_britton.pdf

Chapter Four

1. Leonard, J. (no date) *Juliana Redding, 21 – The Homicide Report, Los Angeles Times*. Los Angeles Times. Available at: https://homicide.latimes.com/post/juliana-redding/ (Accessed: January 22, 2023).
2. *Hollywood Secrets* (no date) *CBS News*. CBS Interactive. Available at: https://www.cbsnews.com/news/48-hours-probes-murder-of-juliana-redding-a-hollywood-whodunit/ (Accessed: January 22, 2023).
3. www.crimelibrary.org. (n.d.). *Hollywood dreams: The Murder of Juliana Redding – Hollywood Dreams – Crime Library*. [online] Available at: https://www.crimelibrary.org/notorious_murders/classics/juliana_redding/1-hollywood-dreams.html [Accessed 23 Feb. 2023].
4. *Hollywood Secrets* (no date) *CBS News*. Available at: https://www.cbsnews.com/news/48-hours-probes-murder-of-juliana-redding-a-hollywood-whodunit/#:~:text=%E2%80%9CThere's%20plenty%20of%20DNA%20at,much%20DNA%2C%E2%80%9D%20Jackson%20continued. (Accessed: 17 September 2023).
5. *Aspiring Actress Dead in SoCal Murder Mystery*. ABC News. (March 18, 2008) Available at: https://abcnews.go.com/US/story?id=4475114&page=1 (Accessed: 17 September 2023).
6. www.cbsnews.com. (n.d.). *Juliana Redding Murder Case: Confession...or gibberish...on videotape put forth by Kelly Soo Park's defense?* [online] Available at: https://www.cbsnews.com/news/juliana-redding-murder-case-confessionor-gibberishon-videotape-put-forth-by-kelly-soo-parks-defense/ [Accessed 23 Feb. 2023].
7. King, G.C. (no date) *Hollywood dreams: The murder of Juliana redding, Investigation – Hollywood dreams: The Murder of Juliana Redding – Crime Library*. Available at: https://www.crimelibrary.org/notorious_murders/classics/juliana_redding/4-investigation.html (Accessed: 17 September 2023).
8. Keltner, D. (2017) *Sex, power, and the systems that enable men like Harvey Weinstein, Harvard Business Review*. Available at: https://hbr.org/2017/10/sex-power-and-the-systems-that-enable-men-like-harvey-weinstein (Accessed: April 13, 2023).
9. Leonard, J. (2013) *Woman charged with strangling model had no motive, lawyer says, Los Angeles Times*. Los Angeles Times. Available at: https://www.latimes.com/local/lanow/la-me-ln-model-murder-trial-defense-20130522-story.html (Accessed: April 13, 2023).
10. Dolan, M. (2017) *Woman acquitted in slaying of Santa Monica Model may sue police, Court says, Los Angeles Times*. Los Angeles Times. Available at: https://www.latimes.com/local/lanow/la-me-ln-murder-defendant-suit-20170314-story.html (Accessed: January 22, 2023).

Chapter Five

1. *Paynesville Victim speaks out: 'it's time for some answers'* (2016) *CBS News*. Available at: https://www.cbsnews.com/minnesota/news/paynesville-victim-speaks-out-its-time-for-some-answers/ (Accessed: 20 September 2023).
2. Baran, M. and Vogel, J. (2022) *Jared Scheierl, APM Reports*. Available at: https://www.apmreports.org/story/2016/09/13/jared-scheierl (Accessed: 20 September 2023).
3. The Hunt With John Walsh – *Jacob Wetterling Abducted, Missing Since October 22, 1989* (no date) *CNN*. Available at: http://edition.cnn.com/TRANSCRIPTS/1408/31/thwjw.01.html (Accessed: 22 September 2023).
4. Vogel, J. and Baran, M. (2022) *Dan Rassier, APM Reports*. Available at: https://www.apmreports.org/story/2016/09/07/dan-rassier (Accessed: 25 September 2023).

5. APM Reports (2016). *It took nearly 27 years to solve a notorious child abduction. Why?* [online] Apmreports.org. Available at: https://www.apmreports.org/story/2016/12/30/27-years-wetterling-child-abduction.

6. www.youtube.com. (n.d.). *A Current Affair, October 26 1989, Jacob Wetterling, Jill Ireland, Zsa Zsa Gabor and Commercials.* [online] Available at: https://www.youtube.com/watch?v=DCOn-vDVP-U [Accessed 25 Feb. 2023].

7. Marohn, K. (2019) Victim of Wetterling Killer testifies about assault, MPR News. Available at: https://www.mprnews.org/story/2018/10/19/victim-of-wetterling-killer-testifies-about-deep-scars-left-by-assault (Accessed: 25 September 2023).

8. Marohn, K. (2019) *What we know about Heinrich's 1990 arrest, MPR News.* Available at: https://www.mprnews.org/story/2018/09/21/the-wetterling-case-what-we-know-about-heinrich-1990-arrest (Accessed: 25 September 2023).

9. Yesko, P. and Gilbert, C. (2022) *Why law enforcement didn't see that Danny Heinrich killed Jacob Wetterling, Why law enforcement didn't see that Danny Heinrich killed Jacob Wetterling | Missing a Murderer | APM Reports.* Available at: https://www.apmreports.org/story/2018/09/21/why-law-enforcement-didnt-see-danny-heinrich-killed-jacob-wetterling#:~:text=He's%20drunk%2C%20according%20to%20a,suspect%20in%20the%20Paynesville%20assaults. (Accessed: 25 September 2023).

10. (KARE), A.K. 11 S. (2016) *Patty Wetterling: How people can help, kare11.com.* Available at: https://www.kare11.com/article/news/local/patty-wetterling-how-people-can-help/89-313868390 (Accessed: 25 September 2023).

11. Yesko, P. (2022) *Law enforcement comes clean on botched Wetterling investigation, Law enforcement comes clean on botched Wetterling investigation | 'All of us failed' | APM Reports.* Available at: https://www.apmreports.org/episode/2018/09/20/wetterling-investigation-documents (Accessed: 25 September 2023).

12. *Jacob Wetterling Resource Centre* (2023) *Zero Abuse Project.* Available at: https://www.zeroabuseproject.org/victim-assistance/jwrc/ (Accessed: 25 September 2023).

Chapter Six

1. Bowden, M. (2013) *The Body in Room 348, Vanity Fair.* Available at: https://www.vanityfair.com/culture/2013/05/true-crime-elegante-hotel-texas-murder (Accessed: March 28, 2023).

2. News, A. (no date) *What Caused This Man's Mysterious Death in a Texas Hotel Room?, ABC News.* Available at: https://abcnews.go.com/US/caused-mans-mysterious-death-texas-hotel-room/story?id=20656854 (Accessed: 08 October 2023).

3. Bowden, M. D.W. (2013) *True crime: How a mysterious Beaumont, Texas, murder was solved, Vanity Fair.* Available at: https://www.vanityfair.com/culture/2013/05/true-crime-elegante-hotel-texas-murder (Accessed: 11 October 2023).

Chapter Seven

1. www.youtube.com. (n.d.). *The Disappearance of Jerika Binks | True Life Crime.* [online] Available at: https://www.youtube.com/watch?v=drMgWNLJ6xM [Accessed 4 Apr. 2023].

2. Carter, K. (2018) *Where is missing runner Jerika Binks?, Cosmopolitan.* Available at: https://www.cosmopolitan.com/health-fitness/a25362241/find-jerika-binks-utah-missing-women-runners/ (Accessed: 13 October 2023).

3. Hamilton, M. (2017). *Running While Female.* [online] Runner's World. Available at: https://www.runnersworld.com/training/a18848270/running-while-female/.

4. Christensen, R.A. (2018) *Family of missing Utah county woman releases new photos showing her alive and running, KUTV*. KUTV. Available at: https://kutv.com/news/local/family-of-missing-utah-county-woman-releases-new-photos-showing-her-alive-and-running (Accessed: April 16, 2023).

5. Tv, K. (2019) *Human remains identified as those of Jerika Binks, KSLTV.com*. Available at: https://ksltv.com/412078/human-remains-identified-jerika-binks/ (Accessed: April 17, 2023).

6. *2020 NCIC missing person and unidentified person statistics* (2021) *FBI*. FBI. Available at: https://www.fbi.gov/file-repository/2020-ncic-missing-person-and-unidentified-person-statistics.pdf/view (Accessed: April 17, 2023).

7. Zach Sommers, *Missing White Woman Syndrome: An Empirical Analysis of Race and Gender Disparities in Online News Coverage of Missing Persons*, 106 J. Crim. L. & Criminology (2016). https://scholarlycommons.law.northwestern.edu/jclc/vol106/iss2/4

8. *MMIW* (no date) *Native Womens Wilderness*. Available at: https://www.nativewomenswilderness.org/mmiw#:~:text=MURDERED%20%26%20MISSING%20INDIGENOUS%20WOMEN&text=As%20of%202016%2C%20the%20National,has%20only%20reported%20116%20cases. (Accessed: April 17, 2023).

Chapter Eight

1. *Profile: Mi6 Spy Gareth Williams* (2012) *BBC News*. Available at: https://www.bbc.com/news/uk-17790563 (Accessed: 22 October 2023).

2. *MI6 worker Gareth Williams was an 'exceptional' pupil* (2010) *BBC News*. Available at: https://www.bbc.co.uk/news/uk-wales-north-west-wales-11095158 (Accessed: 22 October 2023).

3. Campbell, D. (2012) *GCHQ's Spy Death Riddle Shines Light on UK hacker war, The Register® – Biting the hand that feeds IT*. Available at: https://www.theregister.com/2012/05/03/gareth_williams_inquest/ (Accessed: 22 October 2023).

4. Shaw, D. (2012) *MI6 officer Gareth Williams and the 'missing hours' before his death, BBC News*. Available at: https://www.bbc.co.uk/news/uk-17920204 (Accessed: 22 October 2023).

5. Gordon Rayner, Chief Reporter "Was MI6 spy-in-a-bag Gareth Williams killed by 'secret service dark arts'?" Archived 31 March 2012 at the Wayback Machine, *The Telegraph*, 30 March 2012.

6. Patrick Sawer; Gordon Thomas (22 April 2012). "Secret meeting between MI6 and police hours after discovery of spy Gareth Williams's death". *Daily Telegraph*. London. Archived from the original on 25 April 2012. Retrieved 27 April 2012.

7. Vinter, R. and Sinmaz, E. (2023) *'She's not in the river': diving expert in Nicola Bulley case under the spotlight, The Guardian*. Available at: https://amp.theguardian.com/uk-news/2023/feb/23/nicola-bulley-peter-faulding-diving-expert (Accessed: 23 October 2023).

8. *Gareth Williams inquest: MI6 spy could have shut himself in bag, says expert* (2012) *The Guardian*. Available at: https://www.theguardian.com/world/2012/apr/27/gareth-williams-inquest-mi6-spy-bag (Accessed: 23 October 2023).

9. Kemp, P. (2012) *'credible evidence' MI6 spy died alone, says pathologist, BBC News*. Available at: https://www.bbc.co.uk/news/uk-18177069 (Accessed: 23 October 2023).

10. Cook, A. (2013) *Murder?: The likely story of Gareth Williams, Now Then Sheffield*. Available at: https://nowthenmagazine.com/articles/murder-the-likely-story-of-gareth-

williams#:~:text=Meanwhile%2C%20the%20tabloid%20press%20runs,paid%20male%20 escorts%20for%20sex. (Accessed: 27 October 2023).

11. Shaw, D. (2012) *MI6 officer Gareth Williams and the 'missing hours' before his death, BBC News*. Available at: https://www.bbc.co.uk/news/uk-17920204 (Accessed: 27 October 2023).

12. Davies, C. and Meikle, J. (2012) *Gareth Williams's death was 'criminally mediated', says coroner, The Guardian*. Available at: https://www.theguardian.com/uk/2012/may/02/ gareth-williams-coroner-never-solved (Accessed: 27 October 2023).

13. Gavaghan, J. (2012) *Army veteran claims spy-in-bag could easily have locked himself in Holdall... and proves it with his 16-year-old daughter, Daily Mail Online*. Available at: https://www.dailymail.co.uk/news/article-2141946/Army-veteran-claims-spy-bag-easily-locked-holdall--prove-video.html (Accessed: 27 October 2023).

14. Halliday, J. (2013) *MI6 spy found dead in bag probably locked himself inside, met says, The Guardian*. Guardian News and Media. Available at: https://www.theguardian.com/ uk-news/2013/nov/13/mi6-spy-dead-bag-locked-himself-gareth-williams (Accessed: May 7, 2023).

Chapter Nine

1. Godwin, T. (2023) *How many alligators live in Florida's Lake Seminole?, AZ Animals*. Available at: https://a-z-animals.com/blog/how-many-alligators-live-in-floridas-lake-seminole/ (Accessed: 01 November 2023).

2. Portman, J. (2019) *From the archives: Mike Williams disappears from Lake Seminole in 2000, Tallahassee Democrat*. Available at: https://eu.tallahassee.com/story/news/2015/11/25/ mike-williams-hunter-disappears-lake-seminole-2000/76369968/ (Accessed: 01 November 2023).

3. Disappeared (2022) *Jerry Michael Williams, Disappeared*. Available at: https:// disappearedblog.com/jerry-michael-williams/ (Accessed: 01 November 2023).

4. Corbin, C. (2016) *Where is Mike Williams? mother hopes for break in 16-year-old Cold case, Fox News*. Available at: https://www.foxnews.com/us/where-is-mike-williams-mother-hopes-for-break-in-16-year-old-cold-case (Accessed: 01 November 2023).

5. Portman, J. (2019) *Court records: Fears over Mike Williams case drove 2016 kidnapping by Brian Winchester, Tallahassee Democrat*. Available at: https://eu.tallahassee.com/story/ news/2018/01/24/concern-former-wife-mike-williams-would-provipressure-police-mike-williams-case-motive-2016-kidnappi/1058774001/ (Accessed: 01 November 2023).

6. Portman, J. (2017) *Brian Winchester sentenced to 20 years in prison, Tallahassee Democrat*. Available at: https://eu.tallahassee.com/story/news/2017/12/19/brian-winchester-sentenced-20-years-prison/964750001/#:~:text=In%20an%20emotional%20victim%20 impact%20statement%2C%20a%20frail,spend%20the%20rest%20of%20his%20life%20 in%20prison. (Accessed: 01 November 2023).

7. *Williams v. State*, 314 So. 3d 775 (Fla. Dist. Ct. App. 2021) Williams v. State, 314 So. 3d 775 | Casetext Search + Citator

8. Portman, J. (2019b) *Denise Williams insurance fraud case dropped, daughter gets all assets, Tallahassee Democrat*. Available at: https://eu.tallahassee.com/story/news/2019/07/16/ mike-williams-daughter-awarded-all-assets/1742234001/ (Accessed: 07 November 2023).

Chapter Ten

1. *Key information and statistics about missing* (2023) *Missing People*. Available at: https://www.missingpeople.org.uk/for-professionals/policy-and-research/information-and-research/key-information (Accessed: 29 June 2023).
2. Figueroa, T. (2019) *Attorneys lay out road map for trial in deaths of McStay family members who disappeared in 2010*, *Tribune*. Available at: https://www.sandiegouniontribune.com/news/courts/sd-me-merritt-mcstay-opening-statements-20190107-story.html (Accessed: 09 November 2023).
3. Teri Figueroa, J.W.Feb. 2 (2013) *The MCSTAYS: A lingering mystery*, *Tribune*. Available at: https://www.sandiegouniontribune.com/lifestyle/people/sdut-mcstay-missing-fallbrook-family-2013feb02-story.html (Accessed: 09 November 2023).
4. Tortoise (2019) *CA – joey, summer, Gianni, Joseph Jr., McStay Murders 4 Feb 2010 *trial transcripts – no discussion*, *Websleuths*. Available at: https://www.websleuths.com/forums/threads/ca-joey-summer-gianni-joseph-jr-mcstay-murders-4-feb-2010-trial-transcripts-no-discussion.432120/ (Accessed: 13 November 2023).
5. Dziemianowicz, J. (2023) *'monster' slaughters entire family – mom, Dad, 2 young sons – and buries them in the Desert*, *Oxygen Official Site*. Available at: https://www.oxygen.com/killer-motive/crime-news/mcstay-family-murders-who-killed-them#:~:text=Investigators%20focused%20attention%20again%20on,Charles%20Merritt%2C%20Joseph's%20business%20associate. (Accessed: 14 November 2023).
6. Nelson, J. (2018) *San Bernardino judge delays ruling on bid to exclude key evidence in McStay Family Murder Case*, *San Bernardino Sun*. Available at: https://www.sbsun.com/2018/05/04/san-bernardino-judge-delays-ruling-on-bid-to-exclude-key-evidence-in-mcstay-family-murder-case/ (Accessed: 15 November 2023).
7. Stanley, J.L. (2022) *Two Shallow Graves: The McStay Family Murders*. ID.

Chapter Eleven

1. Colloff, P. (2012) *The innocent man, part one*, *Texas Monthly*. Available at: https://www.texasmonthly.com/true-crime/the-innocent-man-part-one/ (Accessed: 18 November 2023).
2. Smith, E. (2022) *Female murder victims and victim-offender relationship, 2021*, *Bureau of Justice Statistics*. Available at: https://bjs.ojp.gov/female-murder-victims-and-victim-offender-relationship-2021 (Accessed: 23 July 2023).
3. Morton, M. (2015) Getting life: An innocent man's 25-year journey from prison to peace. New York: Simon & Schuster.
4. Colloff, P. (2012b) The innocent man, part Two, Texas Monthly. Available at: https://www.texasmonthly.com/true-crime/the-innocent-man-part-two/ (Accessed: 19 November 2023).
5. Colloff, P. (2013) Mark Alan Norwood found guilty of Christine Morton's murder, Texas Monthly. Available at: https://www.texasmonthly.com/articles/mark-alan-norwood-found-guilty-of-christine-mortons-murder/ (Accessed: 19 November 2023).
6. Lindell, C. (2018) Former prosecutor apologizes to wrongfully convicted man, Statesman. Available at: https://www.statesman.com/story/news/local/2011/11/17/former-prosecutor-apologizes-to-wrongfully/6688818007/ (Accessed: 19 November 2023).
7. Facts for all (no date) Vote Smart. Available at: http://votesmart.org/public-statement/783332/gov-perry-signs-senate-bill-1611-the-michael-morton-act#.WP0GpYjyvIU (Accessed: 19 November 2023).

Sources

Podcasts

Renner, J. (April 2018) The Philosophy of Crime. 1 May 2018

Kelly, E. (October 2017) Southern Fried True Crime. 11 January 2021

Clark T, Beckley F, Kern, J. (June 2020) Solved Murders: True Crime Mysteries. 10 February 2021

Books

Vonnegut, K, *The Sirens of Titan*. Dial Press. (1959)

Cooper, B. (2020) *We keep the dead close: A murder at Harvard and a Half Century of Silence*. Grand Central.

Morton, M. (2015) Getting life: An innocent man's 25-year journey from prison to peace. New York: Simon & Schuster.

Journals

Bumbrah, G.S. (2017) "Cyanoacrylate fuming method for detection of Latent Fingermarks: A Review," *Egyptian Journal of Forensic Sciences*, 7(1). Available at: https://doi.org/10.1186/s41935-017-0009-7.

Sommers, Z, *Missing White Woman Syndrome: An Empirical Analysis of Race and Gender Disparities in Online News Coverage of Missing Persons*, 106 J. Crim. L. & Criminology (2016). https://scholarlycommons.law.northwestern.edu/jclc/vol106/iss2/4

Websites

Serena, K. (2021) *Diane Schuler was the perfect PTA Mom, so why did she kill 8 people with her van?* All That's Interesting, https://allthatsinteresting.com/diane-schuler.

Wrong way tragedy: Supporting first responders (2015) *Rivertown's Daily Voice*, https://dailyvoice.com/new-york/rivertowns/news/wrong-way-tragedy-supporting-first-responders/430461/

Stuever, H. (2011) *TV review: 'There's something wrong with Aunt Diane'*, *The Washington Post*. WP Company. https://www.washingtonpost.com/lifestyle/style/tv-review-theres-something-wrong-with-aunt-diane/2011/07/20/gIQARBkCXI_story.html

James, S.D. (2010) *Husband of Taconic Crash's Diane Schuler Sues N.Y. State*, *ABC News*. ABC News Network. https://abcnews.go.com/Health/taconic-crashes-diane-schuler-super-mom-perfectionist-hbo/story?id=14152213

Settlements reached in 4 Taconic Parkway wrong-way crash lawsuits (2014) CBS News. https://www.cbsnews.com/newyork/news/settlements-reached-in-4-taconic-parkway-wrong-way-crash-lawsuits/

Occam's Razor definition & meaning (no date) *Merriam-Webster*. Merriam-Webster. Available at: https://www.merriam-webster.com/dictionary/Occam%27s%20razor

Merriam Webster. *https://www.merriam-webster.com/dictionary/parsimony* (no date) https://www.merriam-webster.com/dictionary/parsimony.

Partington, V. (2021) *Killer hitchhiker: The murder of Dorothy Donovan, Medium.* Medium. https://veritycreates.medium.com/killer-hitchhiker-the-murder-of-dorothy-donovan-b6c5dfc6d359

Pundir, R. (2022) *Solved mysteries that seem strange even for Us, Ranker.* Ranker. Available at: https://www.ranker.com/list/strange-solved-mysteries/rima-pundir

Farnam Street (2019) *How to use Occam's Razor without getting cut, Farnam Street.* Available at: https://fs.blog/occams-razor/

"Ockham's razor". *Encyclopædia Britannica.* Encyclopædia Britannica Online. 2010. Archived from the original on 23 August 2010.

Summa Totius Logicae, i. 12, cited in "Ockham's Razor" by Paul Newall at *Galilean Library* (25 June 2005)

Mental shortcuts (no date) *National Geographic Society.* https://education.nationalgeographic.org/resource/mental-shortcuts

Cherry, K. (2022) *What is cognitive bias? Verywell Mind.* Verywell Mind. Available at: https://www.verywellmind.com/what-is-a-cognitive-bias-2794963

Stockton, C. (2021) *The murderer who wrote 'kill someone + get away with it' on her bucket list, Thought Catalog.* Available at: https://thoughtcatalog.com/christine-stockton/2021/04/the-murderer-who-wrote-kill-someone-get-away-with-it-on-her-bucket-list/

Vanapalli, V. (2021) *Dana Laskowski murder: Where is Emily Lauenborg now?,* The Cinemaholic. https://thecinemaholic.com/dana-laskowski-murder-where-is-emily-lauenborg-now/

Music student at B.U. Throttled by strangler in apt. Near Square: The Harvard Crimson (1963) *News | The Harvard Crimson.* https://www.thecrimson.com/article/1963/5/9/music-student-at-bu-throttled-by/

Reinhold, Robert (January 18, 1969). "Cambridge Murder Victim Is Recalled as Intelligent and Witty". The New York Times. Retrieved December 29, 2018. Available at https://timesmachine.nytimes.com/timesmachine/1969/01/19/90039924.html?action=click&contentCollection=Archives&module=ArticleEndCTA&region=ArchiveBody&pgtype=article&pageNumber=62

de Saint Phalle, Anne (January 8, 1969). "Grad Student Killed". *The Harvard Crimson.* Retrieved December 30, 2018.

"Services Held for Slain Coed". *Associated Press.* January 9, 1969. Retrieved December 30, 2018 – via Lewiston Evening Journal.

"Cambridge Police Declare Black-out On Britton Case". *The Harvard Crimson.* January 10, 1969. Retrieved December 31, 2022. Available at https://www.thecrimson.com/article/1969/1/10/cambridge-police-declare-black-out-on-britton/

MacNeill, Arianna (November 20, 2018). "Jane Britton, a Harvard graduate student, was found murdered in 1969. Now authorities say they know who did it". *Boston.com.* Retrieved January 2, 2019.

"DNA Used to Identify Man Responsible for 1969 Murder of Jane Britton" (PDF) (Press release). Woburn, Massachusetts: Middlesex County District Attorney's Office. Retrieved December 30, 2022. Available at https://www.middlesexda.com/sites/middlesexda/files/news/press_packet_-_jane_britton.pdf

Leonard, J. (no date) *Juliana Redding, 21 – The Homicide Report, Los Angeles Times.* Los Angeles Times. https://homicide.latimes.com/post/juliana-redding/

Hollywood Secrets (no date) *CBS News.* CBS Interactive. https://www.cbsnews.com/news/48-hours-probes-murder-of-juliana-redding-a-hollywood-whodunit/

www.crimelibrary.org. (n.d.). *Hollywood Dreams: The Murder of Juliana Redding – Hollywood Dreams – Crime Library* https://www.crimelibrary.org/notorious_murders/classics/juliana_redding/1-hollywood-dreams.html

Hollywood Secrets (no date) *CBS News*. Available at: https://www.cbsnews.com/news/48-hours-probes-murder-of-juliana-redding-a-hollywood-whodunit/#:~:text=%E2%80%9CThere's%20plenty%20of%20DNA%20at,much%20DNA%2C%E2%80%9D%20Jackson%20continued.

Aspiring Actress Dead in SoCal Murder Mystery. ABC News. (March 18, 2008) Available at: https://abcnews.go.com/US/story?id=4475114&page=1

Leibowitz, B. *Juliana Redding Murder Case: Confession...or gibberish...on videotape put forth by Kelly Soo Park's defence? (May 14 2013)* www.cbsnews.com https://www.cbsnews.com/news/juliana-redding-murder-case-confessionor-gibberishon-videotape-put-forth-by-kelly-soo-parks-defense/

King, G.C. (no date) *Hollywood Dreams: The Murder of Juliana Redding, Investigation – Hollywood Dreams: The Murder of Juliana Redding – Crime Library*. https://www.crimelibrary.org/notorious_murders/classics/juliana_redding/4-investigation.html

Keltner, D. (2017) *Sex, power, and the systems that enable men like Harvey Weinstein, Harvard Business Review*. https://hbr.org/2017/10/sex-power-and-the-systems-that-enable-men-like-harvey-weinstein

Leonard, J. (2013) *Woman charged with strangling model had no motive, lawyer says, Los Angeles Times*. Los Angeles Times. https://www.latimes.com/local/lanow/la-me-ln-model-murder-trial-defense-20130522-story.html

Dolan, M. (2017) *Woman acquitted in the slaying of Santa Monica Model may sue police, Court says, Los Angeles Times*. Los Angeles Times. https://www.latimes.com/local/lanow/la-me-ln-murder-defendant-suit-20170314-story.html

CBS News, *Paynesville Victim speaks out: 'It's time for some answers'* (2016) https://www.cbsnews.com/minnesota/news/paynesville-victim-speaks-out-its-time-for-some-answers/

Baran, M. and Vogel, J. (2022) *Jared Scheierl, APM Reports*. Available at: https://www.apmreports.org/story/2016/09/13/jared-scheier

CNN. The Hunt With John Walsh – *Jacob Wetterling Abducted, Missing Since October 22, 1989* (no date) http://edition.cnn.com/TRANSCRIPTS/1408/31/thwjw.01.html

APM Reports (2016). https://features.apmreports.org/in-the-dark/season-one/

Marohn, K. (2019) Victim of Wetterling Killer testifies about assault, MPR News. https://www.mprnews.org/story/2018/10/19/victim-of-wetterling-killer-testifies-about-deep-scars-left-by-assault

MPR News: https://www.mprnews.org/story/2018/10/19/victim-of-wetterling-killer-testifies-about-deep-scars-left-by-assault

(KARE), A.K. 11 S. (2016) *Patty Wetterling: How people can help, kare11.com*. Available at: https://www.kare11.com/article/news/local/patty-wetterling-how-people-can-help/89-313868390

Jacob Wetterling Resource Centre (2023) *Zero Abuse Project*. https://www.zeroabuseproject.org/victim-assistance/jwrc/

Bowden, M. (2013) *The Body in Room 348, Vanity Fair*. https://www.vanityfair.com/culture/2013/05/true-crime-elegante-hotel-texas-murder

News, A. (no date) *What Caused This Man's Mysterious Death in a Texas Hotel Room? ABC News*. https://abcnews.go.com/US/caused-mans-mysterious-death-texas-hotel-room/story?id=20656854

Bowden, M. D.W. (2013) *True crime: How a mysterious Beaumont, Texas, murder was solved*, *Vanity Fair*. Available at: https://www.vanityfair.com/culture/2013/05/true-crime-elegante-hotel-texas-murder

Carter, K. (2018) *Where is missing runner Jerika Binks?*, *Cosmopolitan*. https://www.cosmopolitan.com/health-fitness/a25362241/find-jerika-binks-utah-missing-women-runners/

Hamilton, M. (2017). *Running While Female*. [online] Runner's World. https://www.runnersworld.com/training/a18848270/running-while-female/.

Christensen, R.A. (2018) *Family of missing Utah county woman releases new photos showing her alive and running*, *KUTV*. KUTV. https://kutv.com/news/local/family-of-missing-utah-county-woman-releases-new-photos-showing-her-alive-and-running

Tv, K. (2019) *Human remains identified as those of Jerika Binks*, *KSLTV.com*. https://ksltv.com/412078/human-remains-identified-jerika-binks/

2020 NCIC missing person and unidentified person statistics (2021) *FBI*. FBI.https://www.fbi.gov/file-repository/2020-ncic-missing-person-and-unidentified-person-statistics.pdf/view

MMIW (no date) *Native Women Wilderness*. Available at: https://www.nativewomenswilderness.org/mmiw#:~:text=MURDERED%20%26%20MISSING%20INDIGENOUS%20WOMEN&text=As%20of%202016%2C%20the%20National,has%20only%20reported%20116%20cases

Finding Jerika [Facebook] Available at https://www.facebook.com/findingJerika/

BBC News: https://www.bbc.co.uk/search?q=gareth+williams&seqId=0d487560-9d24-11ee-a110-17b7e18bf5a4&d=NEWS_PS

Campbell, D. (2012) *GCHQ's Spy Death Riddle Shines Light on UK hacker war*, *The Register® – Biting the hand that feeds it*. https://www.theregister.com/2012/05/03/gareth_williams_inquest/

Gordon Rayner, Chief Reporter: "Was MI6 spy-in-a-bag Gareth Williams killed by 'secret service dark arts'?" Archived 31 March 2012 at the Wayback Machine, *The Telegraph*

Patrick Sawer; Gordon Thomas (22 April 2012). "Secret meeting between MI6 and police hours after discovery of spy Gareth Williams's death". *Daily Telegraph*. London. Archived from the original on 25 April 2012. Retrieved 27 April 2012.

The Guardian: https://www.theguardian.com/uk/gareth-williams

Cook, A. (2013) *Murder?: The likely story of Gareth Williams*, *Now Then Sheffield* https://nowthenmagazine.com/articles/murder-the-likely-story-of-gareth-williams#:~:text=Meanwhile%2C%20the%20tabloid%20press%20runs,paid%20male%20escorts%20for%20sex

Gavaghan, J. (2012) *Army veteran claims spy-in-bag could easily have locked himself in Holdall... and proves it with his 16-year-old daughter*, *Daily Mail Online*.https://www.dailymail.co.uk/news/article-2141946/Army-veteran-claims-spy-bag-easily-locked-holdall--prove-video.html.

Godwin, T. (2023) *How many alligators live in Florida's Lake Seminole?*, *AZ Animals*.https://a-z-animals.com/blog/how-many-alligators-live-in-floridas-lake-seminole/

Portman, J. (2019) *From the archives: Mike Williams disappears from Lake Seminole in 2000*, *Tallahassee Democrat*.: https://eu.tallahassee.com/story/news/2015/11/25/mike-williams-hunter-disappears-lake-seminole-2000/76369968/

Portman, J. (2019) *From the archives: Mike Williams disappears from Lake Seminole in 2000*, *Tallahassee Democrat*. https://eu.tallahassee.com/story/news/2015/11/25/mike-williams-hunter-disappears-lake-seminole-2000/76369968/

Disappeared (2022) *Jerry Michael Williams, Disappeared*. https://disappearedblog.com/jerry-michael-williams/

Corbin, C. (2016) *Where is Mike Williams? Mother hopes for break in 16-year-old Cold case*, *Fox News*. Available at: https://www.foxnews.com/us/where-is-mike-williams-mother-hopes-for-break-in-16-year-old-cold-case

Tallahassee Democrat https://eu.tallahassee.com/

Williams v. State, 314 So. 3d 775 (Fla. Dist. Ct. App. 2021) Williams v. State, 314 So. 3d 775 | Casetext Search + Citator

Key information and statistics about missing (2023) *Missing People* https://www.missingpeople.org.uk/for-professionals/policy-and-research/information-and-research/key-information

The San Diego Union-Tribune https://www.sandiegouniontribune.com/

Tortoise (2019) *CA – Joey, Summer, Gianni, Joseph Jr., McStay Murders 4 Feb 2010 *trial transcripts – no discussion**, *Websleuths*. https://www.websleuths.com/forums/threads/ca-joey-summer-gianni-joseph-jr-mcstay-murders-4-feb-2010-trial-transcripts-no-discussion.432120/

Dziemianowicz, J. (2023) *'monster' slaughters entire family – mom, Dad, 2 young sons – and buries them in the Desert*, *Oxygen Official Site*. https://www.oxygen.com/killer-motive/crime-news/mcstay-family-murders-who-killed-them#:~:text=Investigators%20focused%20attention%20again%20on,Charles%20Merritt%2C%20Joseph's%20business%20associate

Tortoise (2019) *CA – Joey, Summer, Gianni, Joseph Jr., McStay Murders 4 Feb 2010 *trial transcripts – no discussion**, *Websleuths*. https://www.websleuths.com/forums/threads/ca-joey-summer-gianni-joseph-jr-mcstay-murders-4-feb-2010-trial-transcripts-no-discussion.432120/

Nelson, J. (2018) *San Bernardino judge delays ruling on bid to exclude key evidence in McStay Family Murder Case*, *San Bernardino Sun*. https://www.sbsun.com/2018/05/04/san-bernardino-judge-delays-ruling-on-bid-to-exclude-key-evidence-in-mcstay-family-murder-case/

Oxygen True Crime https://www.oxygen.com/

Nelson, J. (2018) *San Bernardino judge delays ruling on bid to exclude key evidence in McStay Family Murder Case*, *San Bernardino Sun*. https://www.sbsun.com/2018/05/04/san-bernardino-judge-delays-ruling-on-bid-to-exclude-key-evidence-in-mcstay-family-murder-case/

Texas Monthly https://www.texasmonthly.com/true-crime/

Smith, E. (2022) *Female murder victims and victim-offender relationship, 2021, Bureau of Justice Statistics*. https://bjs.ojp.gov/female-murder-victims-and-victim-offender-relationship-2021

Lindell, C. (2018) Former prosecutor apologizes to wrongfully convicted man, *Statesman*. https://www.statesman.com/story/news/local/2011/11/17/former-prosecutor-apologizes-to-wrongfully/6688818007/

Facts for all (no date) Vote Smart. Available at: http://votesmart.org/public-statement/783332/gov-perry-signs-senate-bill-1611-the-michael-morton-act#.WP0GpYjyvIU

Media

Contact (1997) Directed by Robert Zemeckis [film]: Warner Brothers

'Lisa's Pony' (1991) The Simpsons, series three, episode eight. Directed by Carlos Baeza. Written by Matt Groening

A Current Affair, October 26 1989, Jacob Wetterling, Jill Ireland, Zsa Zsa Gabor and Commercials. www.youtube.com. (n.d.). [online] https://www.youtube.com/watch?v=DCOn-vDVP-U

The Disappearance of Jerika Binks | True Life Crime www.youtube.com. (n.d.). [online] Available at: https://www.youtube.com/watch?v=drMgWNLJ6xM

Stanley, J.L. (2022) *Two Shallow Graves: The McStay Family Murders*. ID